All About Blockchain & Crypto for Exporters

Dr. Vijesh Jain

Foreign Trade Consultant, Corporate trainer,
Ex Director, United World School of Business
Ex Dean, IILM Business School

ISBN: 9798879923780
Imprint: Independently published

DEDICATION

I wish to dedicate this book to my distinguished professors at IIFT, New Delhi, who so passionately taught me theoretical aspects of business management way back in 1980s. I also dedicate this book to my numerous B School students, corporate students who have so passionately attended my various Topics and workshops on especially the topics related to How to successfully carry out export business in last 20 years. I am also grateful to my more than 100K working students from 195 countries enrolling to my online courses on Udemy and providing me valuable inputs to refine the contents of this book. I also wish to dedicate this book to my wife and children who supported me wholeheartedly and with contribution to write this book.

CONTENTS

ACKNOWLEDGMENTS

This text is a result of inputs provided by several experts in the field of exports and imports, from industry as well as from academic world. I specially thank *Shri Rakesh Roshan*, Professor and *Shri Amit Kumar Rajvanshi*, Chief Manager-Global Supply Chain, at *Dabur India* for showing the correct path for contents formation for this book through valuable discussions. I am also thankful to my student of International Business *Arshvardhar* for arranging the text in correct order and seeing that layout is correct. Finally I wish to acknowledge the frequent support of *Shri Anil Kumar, Dr. Mukesh Porwal, Prof Navneet Saxena* and *Prof. Deepak Tandon* for their support and constantly guiding me to fine tune the information provided in this book.

INTRODUCTION:

All About Blockchain & Crypto for Exporters: A Comprehensive Guide to Modern Business

Topics 1 and 2:

Welcome to "All About Blockchain & Crypto for Exporters," a pivotal addition to the VJ Exports Mastery Courses Series. In this specialized course, we delve deep into the realms of blockchain technology and cryptocurrencies, collectively known as cryptos, and explore their transformative role in modern business landscapes.

Since their commercial inception in 2008, cryptocurrencies and blockchain technology have evolved to become arguably the most consequential technological innovation since the advent of the internet, as noted by Marc Andreessen. The global adoption of this technology by industries and esteemed organizations like the United Nations has ignited an unprecedented level of interest and intrigue.

Amidst this fervor, Bitcoin, the pioneering and most successful cryptocurrency built on blockchain technology, has emerged as a beacon of innovation, sparking renewed interest in leveraging both the currency and its underlying technology for innovative solutions to societal challenges.

However, beyond the hype and headlines, it is imperative to comprehend the intricacies of blockchain technology and cryptocurrencies within the context of addressing contemporary global challenges. The inclusive nature of this technology offers boundless opportunities for startups and enterprises of all scales across diverse sectors.

In this course, we embark on a comprehensive journey to unravel the complexities of blockchains and cryptocurrencies from multifaceted perspectives, elucidating their profound impact on the global business landscape and social fabric. Our focus extends to a meticulous exploration of Bitcoin, the inaugural commercially launched cryptocurrency, revered as the cornerstone of the crypto ecosystem and widely embraced across the globe.

Whether you're a seasoned exporter seeking to navigate the evolving business terrain or a budding entrepreneur eager to harness the potential of blockchain and crypto technologies, this course equips you with the requisite knowledge and insights to thrive in this dynamic ecosystem.

Join us as we embark on an enlightening exploration of blockchain and crypto for exporters, where innovation converges with enterprise to shape the future of global commerce.

Opening case study: Revolutionizing Humanitarian Aid: UN's World Food Program Adopts Blockchain Technology

Chapter 1: Opening Case Study

Topic 4: Background

In 2017, the United Nations (UN) faced a significant challenge when relief funding leakage and high transaction costs for money transfers to refugees and migrants affected by the Syrian conflict came to light. The UN's World Food Program (WFP), operating supermarkets in refugee camps in Jordan, incurred substantial costs due to transaction fees and partnerships with local banks for its prepaid credit card system.

Enter blockchain technology, renowned for its association with the immensely successful Bitcoin as an international virtual currency. Adopting this technology, the WFP witnessed remarkable savings and a reduction in fraud and fund leakage. In the case of blockchain, refugees' accounts were credited with funds, enabling them to redeem credits for food and supplies at WFP-affiliated supermarkets using iris scanners – all without needing physical wallets. These supermarkets then sold the collected credits back to the UN.

Dubbed 'building blocks' by the UN, the program in Jordan was a resounding success, slashing money transfer fees by nearly 98%, curbing fraud, and streamlining aid distribution for both the WFP and refugees. Inspired by this success, the UN explored further innovative applications of blockchain technology in its international relief programs.

Beyond humanitarian aid, excitement has surged globally regarding blockchain's potential in various social and commercial realms. From smart contracts to land records, elections/e-voting, financial products, international trade and commerce, to faster and cheaper international money transfers, the prospects are vast and promising.

However, alongside its potential benefits, blockchain technology has also attracted notoriety for its misuse by criminals, drug peddlers, and terrorists for money laundering. Some applications, notably cryptocurrency mining operations, have been accused of contributing to global warming, while others have facilitated tax evasion and circumvented local government regulations in financial transactions.

Despite these challenges, governments worldwide are increasingly embracing blockchain technology and formulating national and international policies to govern its use. As the world navigates the complexities and opportunities presented by blockchain, its transformative potential continues to captivate imaginations and drive innovation across diverse sectors.

Opening Case Study:

In the previous episode, I outlined the topics we'll cover in this course, including case studies and real-world examples related to Bitcoin and Blockchain. Today, I want to share a story that sheds light on the remarkable impact of blockchain technology, particularly in humanitarian aid, focusing on the United Nations Food Programme (WFP).

When initiatives operate on a global scale, such as the WFP's efforts, managing funds and preventing leakage becomes a significant challenge. Take, for example, the toll collection system on India's national highways. Despite being a vast network managed by the National Highway Authority of India, leakage of funds remains a persistent issue.

Similarly, the WFP faced challenges in ensuring that funds allocated for humanitarian aid reached those in need without leakage or misuse. When conflict led to the establishment of Syrian refugee camps in

Jordan and elsewhere, the WFP allocated substantial funds. However, it became evident that millions of dollars were being lost, not due to corruption, but due to inefficiencies in the traditional financial system.

Source: UNHCR

To address this, the WFP turned to blockchain technology. By leveraging an intranet and internet-based blockchain network, they revolutionized their aid distribution process. Funds were transferred in cryptocurrency form via blockchain technology, eliminating the need for intermediaries like local banks and drastically reducing transaction costs.

Moreover, the blockchain-based system ensured transparency and accountability. Beneficiaries' identities were securely stored on the blockchain, enabling them to redeem aid through iris-based scans, even if their documents were lost or destroyed. This innovative solution not only prevented leakage but also streamlined the aid distribution process, ensuring that those in need received timely assistance.

The success of this pilot project, dubbed 'building blocks,' prompted the UN to adopt blockchain technology across similar aid programs. It's important to note that the decision to embrace blockchain wasn't just about leveraging technology for the sake of it. Instead, it was a strategic move to address a pressing challenge and achieve the organization's mission more effectively.

Just as the UN utilized blockchain technology to enhance humanitarian aid, organizations worldwide can harness its potential to address complex issues and drive positive change. Whether it's optimizing government services, improving supply chain management, or enhancing financial inclusion, blockchain offers transformative possibilities.

As we delve deeper into our exploration of Bitcoin and Blockchain in this course, let's draw inspiration from the UN's innovative use of technology to make a meaningful impact on people's lives. Through understanding and leveraging blockchain, we can pave the way for a more efficient, transparent, and equitable future.

Topic 6: What does the public think about Bitcoin and Blockchain

Hello everyone, and welcome back to the VJ Exports Mastery Series Course on Bitcoin and Blockchain. In our last episode, we explored how blockchain technology was effectively utilized within the United Nations Food Program, highlighting its potential impact beyond just cryptocurrency. Today, we're delving into the complex realm of public opinion surrounding Bitcoin and blockchain technology.

It's undeniable that Bitcoin has experienced significant growth since its inception, becoming a global phenomenon. However, despite its rise, public sentiment remains deeply divided. This sentiment is not unique to any one country but is rather a global phenomenon. Many people exhibit a sense of ignorance towards blockchain and cryptocurrency, avoiding discussions and news related to them altogether. Whether in articles, print media, or digital platforms, a majority of individuals tend to overlook or dismiss information about crypto, assuming they won't comprehend it. But hey you are not alone. 83% of respondents in a 2015 survey conducted by PwC were "slightly familiar/not at all familiar" with cryptocurrencies (PwC, August 2015)

This widespread lack of understanding contributes to a prevailing negative opinion about cryptocurrency among the general public. Most people simply do not grasp the intricacies of blockchain technology, and even if they attempt to educate themselves, they often find the subject matter too complex to comprehend fully. Consequently, the prevailing sentiment toward crypto remains predominantly unfavorable due to this knowledge gap.

One of the primary reasons behind this negative perception is the difficulty in accessing comprehensive and straightforward information about cryptocurrencies. Blockchain technology, which underpins cryptocurrencies like Bitcoin, is inherently complex, making it challenging for individuals to grasp without proper guidance. Moreover, since cryptocurrency is based on cryptography, a branch of mathematics, many people feel intimidated by its technical nature, further exacerbating the issue.

In essence, the lack of accessible education and the inherent complexity of blockchain and cryptocurrency contribute to widespread ignorance and negativity towards them. However, it's essential to recognize that there are individuals who have taken the time to understand crypto and blockchain, viewing their potential in a positive light. These individuals, often involved in the crypto space in some capacity, appreciate the transformative power of blockchain technology and recognize its potential to revolutionize various industries.

In our next installment, we'll delve deeper into the factors shaping public opinion on Bitcoin and blockchain, exploring common misconceptions and the role of education in fostering a more informed understanding. Thank you for joining me on this exploration of public sentiment towards cryptocurrency and blockchain technology. Stay tuned for more insights in the next part of our discussion.

The lack of accessible education about cryptocurrencies and blockchain technology is one of the primary reasons behind the prevailing negative opinion towards them. This technology is inherently complex, making it challenging for individuals to grasp without proper guidance. Without clear and simple explanations, many people find it difficult to understand the intricacies of crypto and blockchain, leading to widespread ignorance.

Moreover, cryptocurrency is based on cryptography, a branch of mathematics that is intimidating to a large portion of the population. Mathematics, being a subject that many people struggle with, further alienates individuals from engaging with crypto-related concepts. As a result, the majority of people do not hold a positive opinion about cryptocurrencies.

However, those who have taken the time to educate themselves about crypto often view its potential in a positive light. Individuals who are closely involved with cryptocurrencies, either through trading or development, understand the transformative power of blockchain technology. They recognize its ability to revolutionize various industries and drive innovation.

A recent example of the disparity in understanding and perception occurred in India when the government imposed a ban on Bitcoin. This move instilled fear among the public, leading to widespread uncertainty about blockchain technology. However, upon closer examination by the Indian Judiciary, it became evident that the ban was based on a misconception that crypto technology held no significant benefits. In a country like India, which holds a leadership position in the IT sector, stifling innovation through such bans is counterproductive. The Supreme Court intervened, overturning the ban and acknowledging the importance of fostering innovation and startups in the country.

This incident underscores the critical role that education and understanding play in shaping public opinion about cryptocurrencies and blockchain technology. Moving forward, it's imperative to provide accessible and comprehensive education about crypto to dispel misconceptions and foster a more positive perception among the general public. In the next part of our discussion, we'll explore further examples and delve deeper into the factors influencing public opinion on Bitcoin and blockchain. Stay tuned for more insights.

The lack of knowledge about Bitcoin and blockchain often leads to misconceptions and negative opinions among the public. Many people perceive cryptocurrencies as intangible assets, making it difficult for them to trust or understand their value. For instance, when Bitcoin was first introduced in 2009, its price was only a few dollars. Today, its value has skyrocketed to nearly INR 800,000, prompting skepticism and doubt among some individuals. They question how such drastic price fluctuations can occur and fear that cryptocurrencies may be a bubble waiting to burst, causing harm to many.

However, experts argue that these negative perceptions stem from a lack of understanding rather than inherent flaws in cryptocurrencies or blockchain technology. Similar to any new innovation, cryptocurrencies have their share of challenges and dark sides. Blockchain, the underlying technology behind Bitcoin and other cryptocurrencies, also has its loopholes and potential risks.

In this course, we'll delve into the darker aspects of blockchain technology and cryptocurrency, shedding light on the potential pitfalls and vulnerabilities. However, whether these drawbacks outweigh the benefits of widespread adoption is a matter of debate. Despite their imperfections, new technologies often bring about significant advancements and positive changes. Therefore, it's crucial to weigh the risks against the benefits when considering the global adoption of cryptocurrencies and blockchain.

Ultimately, the decision to embrace cryptocurrencies on a global scale requires careful consideration of their potential impact, both positive and negative. As we continue our exploration of Bitcoin and blockchain in this course, we'll delve deeper into these complexities, providing you with a comprehensive understanding of the issues at hand. Stay tuned for more insights and discussions on this fascinating topic.

Understanding the potential of cryptocurrencies like Bitcoin and the underlying blockchain technology is crucial in navigating their impact on our society. Just as the internet revolutionized our daily lives, cryptocurrencies and blockchain have the potential to disrupt traditional systems and reshape our future.

However, it's essential to acknowledge that like the internet, cryptocurrencies and blockchain also have a dark side. The existence of the dark web, a hidden part of the internet used for illicit activities, serves as a reminder of the potential misuse of technology. Similarly, cryptocurrencies have been associated with illegal transactions and scams, highlighting the need for awareness and regulation.

In this course, we'll delve into these darker aspects, exploring the risks and challenges associated with cryptocurrencies and blockchain technology. By understanding these potential pitfalls, we can better navigate the complexities of this evolving landscape.

Despite the challenges, the potential of cryptocurrencies and blockchain technology is immense. They offer a decentralized, secure, and efficient way to conduct transactions and store data, potentially revolutionizing various industries. As businesses and investors continue to recognize the benefits, the growth of cryptocurrencies is inevitable.

Ultimately, the widespread adoption of cryptocurrencies depends on various factors, including technological advancements, regulatory frameworks, and public perception. While there may be obstacles along the way, the transformative potential of cryptocurrencies and blockchain technology cannot be ignored.

As we continue our exploration in this course, we'll delve deeper into the intricacies of cryptocurrencies and blockchain, equipping you with the knowledge to navigate this rapidly evolving landscape. Thank you for joining me on this journey of discovery.

Topic7: The Story of Satoshi Nakamoto - The Mysterious Person Behind Bitcoin

Satoshi Nakamoto, the enigmatic figure behind Bitcoin and blockchain technology, remains shrouded in mystery to this day. Despite the widespread recognition of his pseudonym, the true identity of Satoshi Nakamoto remains unknown, adding to the intrigue surrounding his persona.

In 2008, Satoshi Nakamoto published a groundbreaking research paper introducing the world to blockchain technology. This innovative concept proposed a decentralized system for managing transactions, eliminating the need for centralized financial institutions and regulators. Satoshi's vision emerged in the aftermath of the 2008 global financial crisis, a period marked by widespread economic turmoil and systemic failures within traditional financial institutions.

In various writings, Satoshi Nakamoto criticized the centralized nature of traditional financial systems, highlighting their vulnerability to manipulation and collapse. He argued that the reliance on central authorities for data management and transaction verification posed significant risks to individuals and society as a whole. Satoshi envisioned blockchain technology as a solution to these shortcomings, offering a transparent, secure, and decentralized alternative to traditional financial systems.

The publication of Satoshi's research paper laid the foundation for the development of Bitcoin, the world's first decentralized cryptocurrency. In 2009, Satoshi Nakamoto launched the Bitcoin network, showcasing the practical application of blockchain technology. Bitcoin quickly gained traction, attracting attention from technologists, investors, and enthusiasts worldwide.

Satoshi Nakamoto's decision to remain anonymous adds an air of mystery to his legacy. Speculation regarding his true identity abounds, with numerous individuals and groups claiming to be Satoshi Nakamoto. However, none have been able to conclusively prove their identity, leaving Satoshi's true identity a subject of speculation and debate.

Despite the anonymity surrounding his persona, Satoshi Nakamoto's contributions to the world of technology and finance are undeniable. His visionary ideas and pioneering work laid the groundwork for the development of blockchain technology and cryptocurrencies, revolutionizing the way we think about money, transactions, and data management.

As we continue to explore the story of Satoshi Nakamoto, we'll delve deeper into his motivations, inspirations, and the impact of his groundbreaking work on the world of finance and technology. Join me as we unravel the mystery behind one of the most influential figures in modern history.

Satoshi Nakamoto, the elusive figure behind the creation of Bitcoin, remains a subject of fascination and speculation. While the name Satoshi Nakamoto is widely recognized in the world of cryptocurrency, the true identity of this individual—or group of individuals—remains a mystery.

Despite the popular association with Bitcoin, it's essential to understand that Satoshi Nakamoto's most significant contribution to the world was not the creation of Bitcoin itself. Instead, it was the revolutionary concept of blockchain technology that reshaped the landscape of finance and technology.

Blockchain technology, as introduced by Satoshi Nakamoto in a seminal research paper published in 2008, offered a decentralized, transparent, and secure method of managing transactions. This innovative approach challenged the traditional reliance on centralized financial institutions and regulators, paving the way for a new era of digital currency and decentralized systems.

Bitcoin, the cryptocurrency created by Satoshi Nakamoto in 2009, served as an early demonstration of the potential applications of blockchain technology. By leveraging the computing power of a decentralized network of computers, Bitcoin facilitated peer-to-peer transactions without the need for intermediaries or central authorities.

The introduction of Bitcoin sparked a wave of innovation in the cryptocurrency space, leading to the development of thousands of alternative cryptocurrencies, or altcoins, built on blockchain technology. Despite the proliferation of altcoins, Bitcoin remains the most widely recognized and trusted cryptocurrency, with a market share of over 50%.

The anonymity surrounding Satoshi Nakamoto's identity adds to the intrigue of his story. Despite numerous claims and speculations, the true identity of Satoshi Nakamoto remains elusive. Many have attempted to uncover his identity through research and investigation, but conclusive evidence has yet to emerge.

The decision to remain anonymous was likely a strategic one, considering the potential backlash from governments, financial institutions, and powerful individuals who may have felt threatened by the disruptive nature of blockchain technology and cryptocurrencies. By maintaining anonymity, Satoshi Nakamoto protected both himself and the integrity of the Bitcoin network.

In addition to preserving anonymity, Satoshi Nakamoto's decision to use a pseudonym also underscored the philosophical principles underlying Bitcoin and blockchain technology. Concepts such as decentralization, anonymity, and digital empowerment were fundamental tenets of Satoshi's vision, reflected not only in the technology itself but also in his approach to identity and privacy.

As we continue to explore the story of Satoshi Nakamoto, we'll delve deeper into the motivations, inspirations, and implications of his groundbreaking work. Join me as we unravel the mysteries of one of the most influential figures in the history of finance and technology.

Chapter Conclusion

As we draw the curtains on the first chapter of our journey into the world of Bitcoin and blockchain, we've embarked on a captivating exploration of the origins, implications, and mysteries surrounding these revolutionary technologies.

In this chapter, we delved into the intertwined story of Bitcoin and blockchain, uncovering the visionary contributions of Satoshi Nakamoto—the enigmatic figure behind the creation of Bitcoin. Satoshi Nakamoto's groundbreaking research paper on blockchain technology laid the foundation for a decentralized, transparent, and secure method of managing transactions, challenging the traditional financial landscape and offering a glimpse into the future of digital currency.

Through the creation of Bitcoin, Satoshi Nakamoto provided a tangible example of the transformative potential of blockchain technology, sparking a wave of innovation and experimentation in the cryptocurrency space. Despite the proliferation of alternative cryptocurrencies, Bitcoin remains the undisputed leader, commanding the lion's share of the cryptocurrency market and capturing the imagination of millions worldwide.

Yet, the story of Satoshi Nakamoto remains shrouded in mystery, with his true identity continuing to elude researchers and enthusiasts alike. His decision to remain anonymous underscores the philosophical principles of decentralization and digital empowerment that underpin Bitcoin and blockchain technology, challenging the notion of centralized authority and championing individual privacy and autonomy.

As we reflect on the revelations and insights gained in this chapter, we're reminded of the profound impact that Bitcoin and blockchain have already had on the world—and the boundless possibilities that lie ahead. From revolutionizing finance and commerce to empowering individuals and communities, the potential applications of blockchain technology are as vast as they are transformative.

In the chapters to come, we'll delve deeper into the intricacies of Bitcoin, blockchain, and the broader cryptocurrency ecosystem, exploring their practical applications, technical underpinnings, and societal implications. Join us as we continue our journey into the fascinating world of Bitcoin and blockchain, uncovering the secrets and unlocking the potential of these groundbreaking technologies.

Chapter 2: Understanding Bitcoin and Blockchain

Welcome to the next chapter of our exploration into the fascinating world of Bitcoin and blockchain—Understanding Bitcoin and Blockchain. In this chapter, we'll delve deeper into the concepts of blockchain technology and cryptocurrencies, uncovering their significance, implications, and potential to reshape the global economy and society at large.

In recent years, amidst the rapid advancement of information and communication technology, blockchain technology and cryptocurrencies have emerged as groundbreaking innovations with the potential to revolutionize various aspects of our lives. From finance and commerce to governance and beyond, the applications of blockchain technology and cryptocurrencies are vast and far-reaching.

As renowned venture capitalist Marc Andreessen aptly stated, blockchain technology is hailed as one of the most important inventions since the internet itself. Its decentralized, transparent, and secure nature has captivated the imagination of entrepreneurs, investors, and innovators worldwide, sparking a wave of interest and excitement in its transformative potential.

Moreover, cryptocurrencies, the digital assets powered by blockchain technology, are poised to disrupt the traditional financial landscape, offering new avenues for financial inclusion, innovation, and empowerment. With the increasing acceptance and adoption of cryptocurrencies by businesses and consumers alike, the global economy is witnessing a paradigm shift in the way money is managed, transferred, and exchanged.

In this chapter, we'll unravel the complexities of blockchain technology, exploring its underlying principles, mechanics, and applications. We'll also delve into the world of cryptocurrencies, examining their origins, functionalities, and impact on the global financial ecosystem.

Join us on this enlightening journey as we deepen our understanding of Bitcoin and blockchain, uncovering the transformative power of these revolutionary technologies and their potential to shape the future of our world.

Topic 9: Concept and origins of bitcoin and blockchain, explained

In this segment, we embark on a journey to unravel the concept and origins of Bitcoin and blockchain technology, as outlined in the seminal paper authored by the enigmatic figure known as Satoshi Nakamoto. Delving into the abstract of this groundbreaking paper, we gain invaluable insights into the essence of peer-to-peer electronic cash systems and the innovative solution proposed to address the double-spending problem.

Published under the title "Bitcoin: A Peer-to-Peer Electronic Cash System" in 2008 by an individual or group operating under the pseudonym Satoshi Nakamoto, this paper serves as the foundational document of the Bitcoin protocol. As we dissect the abstract, we encounter the core proposition: the creation of a decentralized digital currency that enables direct online payments between parties without the need for intermediaries.

At the heart of Satoshi Nakamoto's proposal lies a solution to the double-spending problem, a longstanding challenge in digital transactions where the same funds are illicitly spent more than once. By leveraging a peer-to-peer network and employing cryptographic techniques such as digital signatures and hash-based proof-of-work, Nakamoto introduces a mechanism to prevent double spending and ensure the integrity of transactions.

Key to this mechanism is the concept of timestamping transactions through hashing and anchoring them to an immutable chain of blocks, forming the blockchain. This chain serves as a distributed ledger, recording all transactions in a transparent and tamper-resistant manner. Crucially, the inclusion of a proof-of-work algorithm ensures that modifying past transactions would necessitate redoing the computational work of the entire network, making it economically and computationally infeasible to alter the blockchain's history.

By elucidating the intricacies of hash-based proof-of-work and its role in securing the integrity of the blockchain, we gain a deeper appreciation for the technological innovations underpinning Bitcoin and blockchain technology. As we continue our exploration, we'll delve further into the mechanics of blockchain consensus mechanisms, cryptographic hashing, and the decentralized nature of peer-to-peer networks, laying the groundwork for a comprehensive understanding of these transformative technologies.

Join us as we embark on this enlightening journey into the world of Bitcoin and blockchain, unraveling the mysteries of its inception and charting the course for its future impact on society and the global economy

In the intricate world of blockchain technology and Bitcoin, the concept of proof-of-work stands as a formidable barrier against the menace of double spending, ensuring the integrity and immutability of transactions within the decentralized network. In this segment, we delve deeper into the mechanics of proof-of-work and its pivotal role in safeguarding the blockchain against fraudulent activities.

Imagine a scenario where unscrupulous builders attempt to sell the same property to multiple buyers, exploiting the inefficiencies of the existing system. This practice, akin to double spending in digital transactions, undermines trust and integrity. However, Satoshi Nakamoto's ingenious solution, articulated through the concept of proof-of-work, erects formidable barriers against such malfeasance.

At its core, proof-of-work requires substantial computational effort to validate and append transactions to the blockchain, akin to the painstaking process of preparing legal documents for property transactions. Just as gathering signatures and endorsements from various stakeholders deters fraudulent property transactions, the computational complexity of proof-of-work makes duplicating transactions economically and computationally infeasible.

Moreover, Nakamoto's design ensures that the longest chain of validated transactions, generated through the concerted efforts of a vast network of computing nodes, serves as an immutable record of transaction history. This distributed consensus mechanism, underpinned by the collective computational power of honest nodes, safeguards the network against malicious attacks and ensures the integrity of the blockchain.

In essence, the blockchain operates as a self-regulating system, where messages are broadcast and validated on a best-effort basis, and nodes can freely join or exit the network without compromising its integrity. The longest chain, symbolizing the collective effort of honest nodes, serves as the definitive record of transaction history, providing assurance and transparency to all network participants.

As we unravel the intricacies of proof-of-work and its role in securing the blockchain, we gain a deeper appreciation for the ingenious design principles underlying Bitcoin and blockchain technology. Join us as we continue our exploration, deciphering the cryptic language of the blockchain and unlocking its transformative potential for the future of finance and beyond.

In the realm of blockchain technology and Bitcoin, cryptography stands as the bedrock upon which the entire system is built. Cryptography, a mathematical function, generates unique hashes for each block within the blockchain, ensuring the integrity and security of transactions. Central to this system is the concept of proof-of-work, a cryptographic puzzle that must be solved through computational effort to append new blocks to the chain.

Imagine attempting to crack a complex combination lock with billions of possible permutations. The computational power required to guess the correct combination is staggering, making it virtually impossible for a single entity to succeed within a reasonable timeframe. This arduous process, known as proof-of-work, ensures that only valid transactions are added to the blockchain, safeguarding against fraudulent activities such as double spending.

Moreover, the decentralized nature of blockchain technology ensures that no single entity has control over the network. Instead, transactions are validated and recorded by a vast network of computers, each contributing computational power to maintain the integrity of the system. This distributed consensus mechanism, coupled with cryptographic principles, forms the backbone of Bitcoin and blockchain technology.

In simpler terms, think of a small village where transactions are conducted verbally and witnessed by the community. When a villager publicly announces the transfer of land to his son-in-law during a wedding ceremony, the entire community becomes aware of the transaction. Although there are no official documents or regulatory authorities involved, the collective memory of the community serves as a testament to the validity of the transaction. Similarly, in the blockchain, transactions are publicly broadcast and validated by the network, ensuring transparency and immutability without the need for centralized oversight.

Satoshi Nakamoto's groundbreaking paper and the subsequent development of Bitcoin and blockchain technology have heralded a new era of digital innovation. Whether this technology will ultimately benefit humanity remains to be seen, but its revolutionary potential cannot be denied. As we continue to explore the intricacies of Bitcoin and blockchain, we unravel the complexities of a transformative technology that holds the promise of reshaping the future of finance and beyond.

Topic 10: Problem with present system of monetary transactions

In our modern monetary system, transactions are primarily conducted through centralized mechanisms controlled by financial institutions. Whether it's using credit cards, debit cards, or making online payments, one unavoidable aspect of these transactions is the presence of middlemen fees. These fees, often unnoticed by consumers, can significantly inflate the cost of transactions, especially when conducted internationally.

When we engage in international transactions, the impact of middlemen fees becomes more apparent. Converting currency from one form to another incurs hefty commissions, transaction costs, and markup fees imposed by intermediaries. Whether converting US Dollars to Indian Rupees or vice versa, the fees imposed by middlemen can erode a substantial portion of the transaction value.

Even at the domestic level, where transaction volumes are higher, middlemen fees persist, albeit sometimes less prominently. In countries like India, with a vast population and extensive transaction volumes, the impact of these fees may seem less pronounced. However, in smaller countries with lower transaction volumes, domestic transactions can still carry significant middlemen fees due to the higher operating costs borne by financial institutions.

These middlemen fees represent a fundamental inefficiency in the current monetary system. They stem from the centralized nature of financial transactions, where intermediaries facilitate exchanges and charge fees for their services. This reliance on intermediaries not only increases transaction costs but also introduces complexities and delays into the process.

Satoshi Nakamoto, recognizing the shortcomings of the existing monetary system, proposed the concept of cryptocurrency as a decentralized alternative. By leveraging blockchain technology, cryptocurrency transactions eliminate the need for middlemen, allowing for peer-to-peer exchanges without excessive fees or delays. As we delve deeper into the world of Bitcoin and blockchain, we'll explore how this revolutionary technology addresses the challenges posed by the current monetary system, offering a more efficient and transparent alternative for financial transactions.

In addition to the exorbitant middleman fees that plague the current system of monetary transactions, another significant issue arises from concerns regarding security. Entrusting private data to central authorities or private entities poses inherent risks, as the intentions of these third-party trustees cannot be guaranteed to prioritize user safety. Even if they refrain from misusing the data, the centralized storage of sensitive information leaves it vulnerable to hacking attempts. The prevalence of data breaches underscores the severity of this security issue, as hackers exploit vulnerabilities in the system to access and misuse personal data. With numerous incidents highlighting the risks associated with centralized data storage, security remains a pressing concern for users worldwide.

Moreover, the accessibility of the current monetary system presents a major challenge for the millions of individuals who remain unbanked. Despite efforts to increase financial inclusion, a significant portion of the global population—over 2 billion people—lack access to banking services. While initiatives like India's Jan Dhan Yojana have made strides in bringing more individuals into the banking fold, there are still vast numbers of people globally who remain disconnected from the formal financial system. For these individuals, cash remains the primary medium of exchange. However, relying solely on cash poses its own set of challenges, including the risk of theft, the logistical burden of handling physical currency, and the lack of traceability inherent in cash transactions.

In light of these issues, it becomes evident that the current monetary system is rife with inefficiencies and vulnerabilities. From exorbitant fees and security concerns to accessibility limitations, the shortcomings of the existing system underscore the need for alternative solutions. In the following sections, we will explore how Bitcoin and blockchain technology offer a promising avenue for addressing these challenges, providing a decentralized, secure, and accessible framework for conducting financial transactions.

Topic 11: Improved monetary transaction system using block-chain: Crypto currencies

Cryptocurrencies, built on blockchain technology, offer a compelling solution to the inefficiencies and vulnerabilities inherent in the traditional monetary transaction system. The decentralized nature of cryptocurrencies eliminates the need for intermediaries, such as banks and credit card companies, significantly reducing transaction costs.

Unlike conventional transactions, where middlemen fees can add up to substantial amounts, cryptocurrency transactions typically incur only minimal mining fees, compensating those who contribute to the blockchain network's security and integrity through proof-of-work.

Moreover, the use of cryptocurrencies can dramatically reduce transaction costs, particularly on an international scale. Traditional methods of transferring funds internationally often involve exorbitant fees, as exemplified by the United Nations' challenges in disbursing funds to Syrian refugee camps. However, by leveraging blockchain-based cryptocurrencies, organizations can bypass costly intermediaries and streamline the transfer process, saving millions of dollars in the process.

Furthermore, cryptocurrencies offer a digital alternative to traditional cash transactions, eliminating the logistical challenges associated with handling physical currency. With cryptocurrencies, transactions can be conducted entirely online, overcoming barriers of tangibility and accessibility. Even individuals without access to traditional banking services can participate in the digital economy, as cryptocurrencies only require an internet connection and a mobile device.

Additionally, the inherent security features of blockchain technology ensure the integrity and privacy of cryptocurrency transactions. By utilizing cryptographic protocols, cryptocurrencies offer enhanced privacy and anonymity, shielding users' personal data from unauthorized access. While some governments may impose regulations to mitigate concerns surrounding anonymity, blockchain's decentralized architecture limits the involvement of private entities, enhancing data security for users.

In summary, cryptocurrencies represent a transformative advancement in monetary transactions, offering a decentralized, cost-effective, and secure alternative to traditional banking systems. By harnessing the power of blockchain technology, cryptocurrencies have the potential to revolutionize the way individuals and organizations conduct financial transactions, paving the way for a more inclusive and efficient global economy.

Chapter conclusion

In conclusion, the exploration of cryptocurrencies and blockchain technology reveals a paradigm shift in the landscape of monetary transactions. From the origins of Bitcoin and blockchain to the challenges inherent in the present system of monetary transactions, we've delved into the fundamental flaws and inefficiencies that plague traditional banking systems. However, the emergence of cryptocurrencies offers a promising solution to these shortcomings.

Cryptocurrencies, built upon the decentralized framework of blockchain technology, present a compelling alternative to traditional monetary systems. By eliminating intermediaries and reducing transaction costs, cryptocurrencies streamline financial transactions, particularly on an international scale. Moreover, the digital nature of cryptocurrencies transcends the limitations of physical cash, offering accessibility to the unbanked population and simplifying the transfer process.

Furthermore, the security features embedded within blockchain technology ensure the integrity and privacy of cryptocurrency transactions. Through cryptographic protocols, cryptocurrencies safeguard users' personal data, offering enhanced privacy and anonymity. Despite regulatory challenges surrounding anonymity, blockchain's decentralized architecture minimizes the involvement of private entities, thereby enhancing data security.

As we navigate through the complexities and potentials of cryptocurrencies, it becomes evident that they represent a transformative force in the realm of monetary transactions. By harnessing the power of blockchain technology, cryptocurrencies have the capacity to revolutionize the global economy, fostering inclusivity, efficiency, and security in financial transactions.

Looking ahead, the widespread adoption of cryptocurrencies holds the promise of a more equitable and accessible financial landscape. However, it is imperative to address regulatory concerns and technological barriers to ensure the responsible and sustainable integration of cryptocurrencies into mainstream financial systems. With continued innovation and collaboration, cryptocurrencies have the potential to reshape the future of finance, empowering individuals and organizations alike in the digital age.

Discussion Questions:

1. Reflecting on the historical context provided regarding the evolution of currency and financial systems, what parallels do you see between past innovations like the agricultural revolution and the emergence of blockchain technology?

2. Considering the dark sides of cryptocurrencies discussed, such as environmental concerns and potential security risks, how might these factors impact public perception and adoption of blockchain technology in mainstream industries?

3. Building on the discussion of the Industrial Revolution and its environmental impacts, how can we apply lessons from history to address the sustainability challenges posed by cryptocurrency mining and blockchain technology?

4. Discuss the role of government regulation and oversight in addressing the dark sides of cryptocurrencies and ensuring responsible innovation in the blockchain space. How can policymakers strike a balance between fostering innovation and protecting consumer interests?

5. Reflecting on the concept of decentralization and its implications for traditional financial systems, what opportunities and challenges do you foresee for banks and financial institutions in adapting to the rise of decentralized finance (DeFi) and blockchain-based currencies?

6. Considering the potential for blockchain technology to democratize access to financial services, how might it contribute to financial inclusion and empowerment, particularly in underserved communities and developing regions?

7. Discuss the role of education and awareness in promoting understanding and adoption of blockchain technology. What steps can

be taken to bridge the knowledge gap and promote digital literacy among businesses and consumers?

8. Building on the discussion of smart contracts and blockchain applications in supply chain management, how might these innovations streamline operations, reduce costs, and enhance transparency in global trade and commerce?

9. Reflecting on the ethical considerations raised by the use of blockchain technology, such as data privacy and security, how can businesses and organizations ensure responsible and ethical use of blockchain solutions?

10. Considering the broader societal implications of blockchain technology, including its potential to disrupt industries and reshape economic systems, what opportunities and challenges do you foresee for individuals, businesses, and society as a whole in embracing blockchain innovation?

Chapter 3: Dealing in Bitcoin and other Cryptocurrencies

In this chapter, we delve into the fascinating world of dealing in Bitcoin and other cryptocurrencies, exploring the intricate landscape of user interfaces and their pivotal role in navigating the realm of digital currencies. As the popularity of cryptocurrencies continues to surge, understanding how users interact with these decentralized financial systems becomes increasingly crucial. From navigating trading platforms to managing digital wallets, the user's computer interface serves as the gateway to a myriad of transactions and investments in the crypto space. Join us as we unravel the complexities of dealing in Bitcoin and other cryptocurrencies, examining the tools, techniques, and strategies essential for navigating this ever-evolving landscape with confidence and clarity.

Topic 12: How to manage bitcoin account online?

In the realm of managing a Bitcoin account online, the user interface plays a pivotal role in facilitating transactions and ensuring security. To embark on this journey, users typically begin by accessing a Bitcoin exchange platform. Similar to the familiarity of online banking interfaces, these exchanges provide a seamless environment for users to buy, sell, and trade cryptocurrencies.

However, one notable distinction lies in the complexity of user identification. Instead of conventional usernames, Bitcoin users are assigned lengthy, alphanumeric addresses known as private keys. These private keys serve as the gateway to the user's account and are crucial for generating unique addresses for transactions. Unlike traditional login credentials, safeguarding the private key becomes paramount, as it holds the key to accessing and managing the account.

Furthermore, the private key operates as a cryptographic tool, employing mathematical functions to secure transactions. This inherent layer of security ensures the integrity and authenticity of each transaction, enhancing user confidence in the system.

Unlike centralized banking systems, Bitcoin transactions operate on a decentralized network, free from the constraints of a central authority's database. This decentralized nature not only empowers users with greater control over their funds but also underscores the fundamental difference between traditional monetary systems and the innovative world of digital currencies.

In the next part, we will delve deeper into the intricacies of managing Bitcoin accounts online, exploring additional security measures and best practices for seamless transaction management. Stay tuned as we unravel the mysteries of digital finance in the realm of cryptocurrencies.

Navigating the landscape of managing a Bitcoin account online unveils several nuances unique to the world of cryptocurrencies. One notable distinction lies in the absence of traditional banking fees, such as credit card charges or intermediary fees. Instead, users encounter a nominal mining fee, which fluctuates depending on network activity. Despite this variability, the mining fee remains insignificant for moderate to high-value transactions, rendering it a negligible consideration for users engaged in sizable transactions.

Unlike traditional monetary systems, where transaction costs often correlate with transaction volume, Bitcoin transactions operate independently of transaction size. This departure from conventional models underscores the decentralized nature of cryptocurrencies, where market forces, rather than centralized authority, dictate pricing dynamics. Consequently, the demand-supply dynamics of cryptocurrencies can precipitate rapid and substantial price fluctuations, challenging users to make swift and informed decisions amidst volatile market conditions.

The inherent volatility of cryptocurrencies serves as a double-edged sword, fostering rapid price appreciation alongside the risk of significant value depreciation. Unlike fiat currencies subject to centralized oversight, cryptocurrencies operate as untamed entities, prone to swift and unpredictable movements akin to an unbridled horse. While this volatility presents opportunities for profit, it also exposes users to considerable risk, highlighting a critical aspect of the cryptocurrency landscape.

In the next part of our exploration, we will delve deeper into strategies for mitigating the risks associated with cryptocurrency volatility, equipping users with the knowledge and tools needed to navigate this dynamic landscape effectively. Stay tuned as we uncover essential insights into managing Bitcoin accounts online amidst fluctuating market conditions.

Topic 13: Example of Bitcoin interface for sending and receiving

When engaging with Bitcoin interfaces for sending and receiving transactions, users encounter a streamlined process facilitated by cryptocurrency exchanges like Bitrex or CoinBase. Let's explore a practical example of the user interface for sending Bitcoin transactions.

Imagine you intend to send approximately $99.9 to a recipient. Upon accessing the Bitcoin exchange interface, you'll observe an intuitive platform resembling that of online banking. To initiate the transaction, you'll need the recipient's Bitcoin address—a lengthy alphanumeric string serving as their unique identifier.

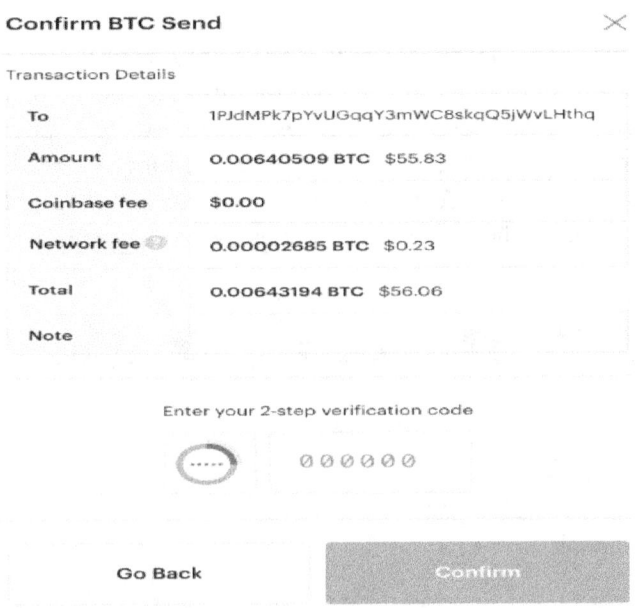

In the example provided, the transaction incurs no mining fee, denoted by a zero BTC fee, offering a notable advantage over traditional banking systems. This feature remains consistent regardless of transaction volume, ensuring a uniform and negligible network fee—$0.23 in this instance, irrespective of the transaction's dollar value.

As you navigate the interface, you'll observe essential details such as the transaction completion status, transaction date, and time. Notably, there's no requirement to input the recipient's personal information or bank account details, preserving user anonymity and data security.

Another compelling aspect is the real-time price updates against the dollar, reflecting the dynamic nature of cryptocurrency markets. Despite the volatility inherent in cryptocurrencies, transactions remain swift and efficient, underscored by their decentralized and secure nature.

In summary, managing Bitcoin transactions online offers users unparalleled convenience, anonymity, and cost-effectiveness. Through intuitive interfaces and minimal transaction fees, cryptocurrency exchanges empower users to navigate the digital economy seamlessly.

Topic 14: Buying and selling of cryptocurrencies on Coinbase

Welcome back to another insightful episode of the VJ Exports Mastery Series Course, where we delve deeper into the world of Bitcoin and Blockchain. In our last session, we explored the advantages of cryptocurrencies and highlighted the shortcomings of traditional cash management systems. Today, we'll expand our knowledge by focusing on buying and selling cryptocurrencies, with a special emphasis on Coinbase.

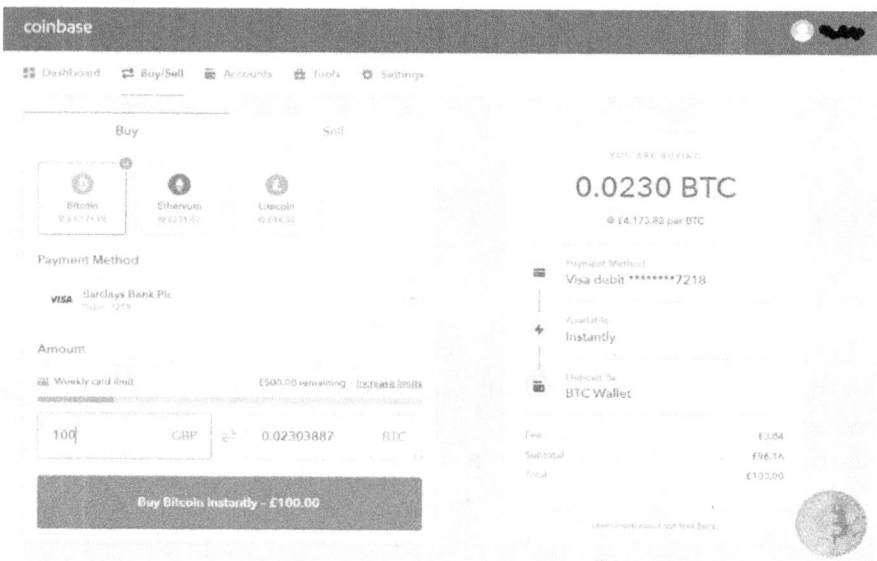

To engage in the buying and selling of cryptocurrencies like Bitcoin, you'll need a dedicated Bitcoin wallet. Coinbase is a popular choice among several cryptocurrency exchanges where you can create and manage your Bitcoin wallet seamlessly.

Upon accessing the Coinbase dashboard, you'll find a user-friendly interface designed for effortless transactions. Here, you have the option to buy or sell cryptocurrencies with just a few clicks. Coinbase supports transactions not only for Bitcoin but also for other leading cryptocurrencies like Ethereum and Litecoin, offering users a diversified portfolio to explore.

When initiating a purchase, you have the flexibility to link your payment method to a credit card or a traditional bank account. Simply input the desired amount in your preferred currency, whether it's dollars, British pounds, or Euros, and Coinbase will provide you with the equivalent amount of Bitcoin based on the current exchange rate.

Let's consider an example: You decide to purchase 0.023 Bitcoin for 100 British Pounds. At the prevailing exchange rate of 4174 pounds per Bitcoin, Coinbase executes the transaction and charges a nominal network fee of 3.84 pounds. Consequently, the subtotal amounts to 96.1 pounds, reflecting the converted value of Bitcoin in your wallet.

In essence, Coinbase offers a straightforward method for users to buy and sell cryptocurrencies, providing access to a diverse range of digital assets and facilitating seamless transactions across multiple currencies. With Coinbase, you can easily navigate the dynamic world of cryptocurrency trading with confidence and convenience.

Topic 15: How to create a crypto currency wallet in India

In this section, we'll explore the process of creating a cryptocurrency wallet in India, offering step-by-step guidance to help you navigate through this essential aspect of cryptocurrency management. While the focus is on India, the fundamental steps are applicable in various other countries, providing a comprehensive understanding of the wallet creation process.

Firstly, it's crucial to select the type of cryptocurrency wallet that best suits your requirements. There are several types available, including hardware wallets, software wallets (which can further be categorized into desktop, mobile, and web wallets), and paper wallets. Each type has its unique features and advantages, so it's essential to explore them in detail to make an informed decision.

Popular wallet options include Coinbase, Trust Wallet, MetaMask, and Ledger Nano S, each offering distinct features and functionalities. Coinbase, for instance, is renowned worldwide for its user-friendly interface and extensive range of supported cryptocurrencies.

The next step involves conducting thorough research on the selected wallet options. Security should be a primary consideration, so it's essential to assess the security features of each wallet carefully. Additionally, evaluate factors such as user interface, reviews, and supported cryptocurrencies to ensure compatibility with your needs and preferences.

Understanding the relationship between wallets and exchanges is also crucial. Many wallets are directly linked to cryptocurrency exchanges, facilitating seamless transactions. Therefore, it's essential to verify whether the chosen wallet is compatible with your preferred exchange platform.

Once you've made your selection, visit the official website or page of the wallet provider to download the wallet application. After downloading the application, proceed to sign up and create your account. During the registration process, you'll be required to provide necessary information, such as your email ID and password.

In India, compliance with Know Your Customer (KYC) and Anti-Money Laundering (AML) regulations is mandatory for cryptocurrency transactions. Therefore, be prepared to submit identification documents, such as your PAN card, TIN number, or Aadhaar card, to complete the KYC verification process.

By following these steps diligently, you'll successfully create your cryptocurrency wallet, enabling you to engage in secure and efficient cryptocurrency transactions within the Indian market and beyond. Stay tuned for the next part, where we'll delve deeper into the process of managing your cryptocurrency wallet effectively.

After successfully creating your cryptocurrency wallet, the next crucial step is to ensure its security. One of the simplest and most effective security measures is enabling two-factor authentication (2FA), especially for web-based or online wallets. By enabling 2FA, you add an additional layer of protection to your account, enhancing its security against unauthorized access.

Furthermore, it's imperative to take immediate action to safeguard your wallet by creating a backup. Most common wallets provide a recovery phrase, also known as a seed phrase, during the setup process. This phrase is essential for restoring access to your wallet in case you encounter any issues, such as forgetting your password or being unable to access your account for any reason. Be sure to write down this recovery phrase and store it securely, as it serves as a vital tool for account recovery.

In many cases, identity verification is required to verify your account, especially in India, where regulatory compliance is mandatory. This verification process may involve providing personal information, such as your PAN card or Aadhaar card, and is necessary for linking your wallet to your bank account or conducting large transactions.

Once your wallet is verified and secured, the next step is to fund it. You can add funds to your wallet by purchasing cryptocurrency directly through the wallet (if supported), transferring cryptocurrency from another account or exchange, or receiving funds from others.

It's important to stay informed about the regulatory landscape of cryptocurrency in India, as regulations may evolve over time. Keeping abreast of these changes ensures compliance with government regulations and helps you navigate the cryptocurrency space responsibly.

Finally, remember that your cryptocurrency wallet consists of two essential components: the public key and the private key. The public key is used for receiving funds and can be shared publicly, while the private key serves as your password and must be kept confidential to protect your funds and ensure the security of your wallet.

In conclusion, thorough research is essential before opening a cryptocurrency account, particularly regarding security features, fees, supported currencies, and user reviews. By following these steps and maintaining a proactive approach to security, you can create a safe and secure environment for buying and selling cryptocurrencies.

Topic 16: Types of Crypto Currencies Wallets

Understanding the different types of cryptocurrency wallets is crucial for selecting the one that best suits your needs and provides the desired level of security. The main types of cryptocurrency wallets include hardware wallets, software wallets, and paper wallets. Let's delve into each type to understand its features and benefits.

Hardware wallets are physical devices that store cryptocurrencies offline. These wallets utilize specialized hardware components to securely store digital assets. One of the key advantages of hardware wallets is their high level of security. Since they operate offline, they are immune to hacking attacks, web-based threats, and online breaches. Users typically pay a one-time fee ranging from $50 to $200 to acquire hardware wallets. Examples of popular hardware wallets available in India include Ledger Nano S and Ledger Nano X, as well as Trezor. Hardware wallets are ideal for long-term storage and safeguarding large volumes of cryptocurrency.

On the other hand, **software wallets** are digital applications that can be installed on desktop or laptop computers. While they provide more security compared to online wallets, software wallets are still susceptible to online attacks. However, they offer greater convenience and accessibility for everyday use. Some common examples of desktop wallets include Exodus, Electrum, and Atomic wallet.

Mobile wallets, another type of software wallet, are mobile applications that can be installed on smartphones. These wallets offer unparalleled convenience, allowing users to perform transactions on the go. While mobile wallets may not provide the same level of security as hardware wallets, they are suitable for users who prioritize accessibility and ease of use. Popular mobile wallets include Trust Wallet, Coinbase wallet, and MetaMask mobile wallet.

Each type of cryptocurrency wallet has its own set of features, advantages, and limitations. Therefore, it's essential to assess your requirements and preferences before choosing the most suitable wallet type for your needs. Whether you prioritize security, convenience, or accessibility, there is a cryptocurrency wallet available to meet your specific requirements.

The third type of software wallet is the **online or web-based wallet**, which can be accessed from any device with internet connectivity. While these wallets offer convenience, they also pose higher risks compared to hardware or desktop wallets due to the possibility of hacking attacks. Examples of online wallets include Coinbase, Binance, and MyEtherWallet (MEW). Despite their convenience, users should exercise caution and prioritize security when using online wallets.

Paper wallets are another type of cryptocurrency wallet that provides offline storage by printing the public and private keys on a physical document. Although paper wallets offer enhanced security by being completely offline, they require careful handling and storage to prevent physical damage or loss. Users may opt to store scanned copies of paper wallets for added security.

Multi-signature wallets, on the other hand, operate on the basis of multiple private keys, requiring authorization from multiple parties to execute transactions. These wallets are particularly useful for organizations or groups dealing in cryptocurrency transactions, providing enhanced security and accountability. For example, multinational companies involved in international trade may utilize multi-signature wallets to ensure secure and transparent transaction management.

Custodial wallets, also known as third-party wallets, are managed by third-party service providers who oversee the storage and management of cryptocurrency funds on behalf of users. While custodial wallets offer convenience and portfolio management services, users must entrust their private information and funds to third parties, raising security concerns. Examples of custodial wallets include exchanges like Coinbase, Binance, and Kraken, which offer wallet management services alongside trading platforms.

Each type of cryptocurrency wallet has its own set of features, advantages, and considerations. Users should carefully assess their security requirements, preferences, and trust levels before selecting a suitable wallet type for their cryptocurrency storage and transaction needs. Whether prioritizing security, convenience, or functionality, there is a cryptocurrency wallet available to meet the diverse needs of users in the digital asset ecosystem.

Topic 17: How to choose the best wallet suitable to your needs?

Choosing the best cryptocurrency wallet for your needs requires careful consideration of various factors, primarily centered around your specific requirements and priorities. Security is often the foremost concern, especially when dealing with substantial funds or long-term storage. Hardware and paper wallets offer the highest level of security, making them ideal choices for individuals seeking maximum protection. While hardware wallets entail a one-time purchase fee, they provide offline storage of cryptocurrency, safeguarding it from online threats.

Conversely, if convenience and ease of use are your primary concerns, mobile or online wallets, also known as web-based wallets, may be more suitable. These wallets offer flexibility and accessibility, allowing users to manage their funds from any device with internet connectivity. However, they may pose higher security risks compared to hardware wallets due to their online nature.

For active traders or those engaging in frequent buying and selling of cryptocurrencies, exchange-provided wallets integrated with trading features may be preferable. While these wallets may lack the same level of security as hardware wallets, they offer convenience and functionality tailored to trading activities. Additionally, custodial wallets provided by exchanges or third-party service providers can be utilized, provided users trust the platform's security measures.

Ultimately, the best wallet for you depends on your individual needs, risk tolerance, and preferences. Conducting thorough research, understanding the security features and reputation of different wallet options, and assessing your security requirements are essential steps in selecting the most suitable wallet. By carefully evaluating these factors, you can make an informed decision and choose a wallet that aligns with your priorities and offers the necessary security for your cryptocurrency holdings.

Topic 18: Active trading in cryptocurrency based from India

When engaging in active trading of cryptocurrencies in India, it's essential to familiarize yourself with the most popular exchanges available. While I won't explicitly recommend any exchange, conducting thorough research on their features, fees, and security measures is crucial before making a decision. Here are some examples of prominent exchanges in India:

1.   WazirX: Recently acquired by Binance, WazirX is known for its user-friendly platform and support for various cryptocurrencies. It typically charges a maker fee (for creating liquidity) and a taker fee (for taking liquidity), ranging from 0.1% to 0.2% per transaction.

2.   CoinDCX: The fee structure on CoinDCX depends on your trading volume and market activity. It also applies maker and taker fees, with rates starting from 0.1% and ranging up to 0.15% to 0.25% per transaction.

3.   BitBNS: BitBNS is popular for its diverse range of supported cryptocurrencies and user-friendly interface. It charges a flat fee of 0.25% per transaction, regardless of whether you're a maker or a taker.

4.   UnoCoin: UnoCoin is known for its simplicity, but it may have slightly higher fees compared to other exchanges. Fees can go as high as 0.7% for both buy and sell transactions.

5.   Jeb Pay: Previously operating outside India due to regulatory changes, Jeb Pey has now returned to the Indian market with a user-friendly interface. Its fees typically range from 0.15% to 0.25% per transaction.

Before choosing an exchange, consider factors beyond just transaction fees. Evaluate the platform's demo, security measures, customer support, ease of use, available trading pairs, deposit and withdrawal methods, and overall reputation for reliability and compliance with Indian government regulations. Conducting thorough research and seeking advice from experienced traders can help you make an informed decision suited to your trading needs and preferences.

Topic 19: Common wallets these exchanges are integrated with

When discussing common wallets associated with exchanges in India, it's important to understand the types of wallets available and their integration with these platforms. Let's delve into the details:

1.   Exchange Wallets: Exchange wallets are built-in wallets provided by cryptocurrency exchanges. These wallets support the currencies listed on the exchange and are offered to users upon creating an account. They are primarily designed for buying and selling cryptocurrencies within the exchange platform. Users can choose to use these wallets exclusively for transactions on the specific exchange.

2.   External Software Wallets: Users can integrate external software wallets with cryptocurrency exchanges. These wallets include mobile wallets like Trust Wallet and MetaMask, as well as desktop wallets such as Exodus and Electrum. Users can generate wallet addresses within these software wallets and use them to deposit or withdraw cryptocurrencies from the exchange. It's essential to ensure that the exchange supports the specific software wallet chosen by the user.

3.   Hardware Wallets Integration: Cryptocurrency exchanges also offer integration with hardware wallets like Ledger Nano S, Ledger Nano X, and Trezor. Users with significant cryptocurrency holdings often prefer hardware wallets for enhanced security. Integration allows users to securely deposit and withdraw funds from the exchange using their hardware wallet addresses, which store crypto funds offline.

4.   Custodial Wallets: Custodial wallets are maintained by third-party service providers or exchanges themselves. Users who opt for custodial wallets entrust the management of their crypto funds to these platforms. Integration with custodial wallets is inherent to the exchange platform, and users can directly transfer funds without managing private keys. It's crucial to consider the reputation and security

measures of custodial wallet providers before entrusting them with your crypto assets.

The integration of wallets varies among exchanges, and it's essential to conduct thorough research before selecting an exchange. Factors to consider include supported wallets, deposit and withdrawal options, transaction fees, and security measures. Prioritizing security and opting for reputable wallets are paramount when storing and managing cryptocurrency assets. Always choose wallets that prioritize user security and offer transparent services to ensure the safety of your funds.

Topic 20: Examples of popular wallets in India

Here are some popular wallets commonly used in India:

1. Exchange Wallets:

   - WazirX: Known for its user-friendly platform and support for various cryptocurrencies.
   - CoinDCX: Offers diverse crypto support and features for trading.
   - BitBNS: Supports a wide range of cryptocurrencies and provides a user-friendly platform.
   - Unocoin: Known for its simplicity and user-friendly interface.
   - ZebPay: Provides its own exchange wallet with user-friendly features.

2. External Software Wallets:

   - Trust Wallet: A mobile wallet offering secure storage and ease of use.
   - MetaMask: Popular for browser-based transactions and Ethereum-based tokens.
   - Coinomi: Offers support for multiple cryptocurrencies and boasts strong security features.
   - Exodus: A desktop wallet known for its intuitive interface and support for various assets.

- Electrum: A desktop wallet focusing on speed and simplicity in Bitcoin transactions.
- Atomic Wallet: Offers a wide range of supported assets and decentralized features.

3. Hardware Wallets:

- Ledger Nano S: A popular hardware wallet offering offline storage and robust security.
- Ledger Nano X: The upgraded version of Ledger Nano S with added features and support.
- Trezor Model T: Known for its advanced security features and ease of use.
- Trezor One: An affordable hardware wallet providing secure storage for cryptocurrencies.

4. Custodial Wallets:

Some exchanges offer custodial wallet services where users can store their cryptocurrencies directly on the exchange platform. Examples include Coinbase, Binance, and Kraken.

When selecting a wallet, consider factors such as supported currencies, security features, user interface, and compatibility with your preferences and needs. Prioritize security measures like two-factor authentication, especially for software wallets. Ensure to safeguard your private keys and conduct thorough research before choosing a wallet. You can refer to the resource section for a comprehensive list of exchanges and wallets mentioned in this Topic, along with step-by-step procedures for reference.

Chapter Conclusion

In conclusion, understanding cryptocurrency wallets and exchanges is essential for anyone venturing into the world of digital assets. Throughout this chapter, we delved into various aspects of cryptocurrency wallets, exchanges, and trading practices in India.

We explored the different types of cryptocurrency wallets, including hardware wallets, software wallets (such as desktop, mobile, online/web-based, and paper wallets), multi-signature wallets, and custodial wallets. Each type has its own set of features, security measures, and suitability for different needs and preferences.

Furthermore, we discussed how to choose the best wallet based on individual requirements, emphasizing the importance of security, convenience, and long-term goals. Whether opting for hardware wallets for maximum security, software wallets for ease of use, or custodial wallets for managed services, users must prioritize security measures and conduct thorough research before making a decision.

We also examined the active trading landscape in India, highlighting popular cryptocurrency exchanges like WazirX, CoinDCX, BitBNS, Unocoin, and ZebPay. Understanding the fee structures, security measures, and trading features of these exchanges is crucial for anyone engaging in cryptocurrency trading activities.

Additionally, we explored common wallets integrated with these exchanges, including exchange wallets offered by the platforms themselves, external software wallets, hardware wallets, and custodial wallets. Users must consider factors such as supported currencies, security features, and ease of use when choosing a wallet for their cryptocurrency transactions.

In conclusion, navigating the world of cryptocurrency wallets and exchanges requires careful consideration, research, and adherence to security best practices. By understanding the different types of wallets, choosing the best option based on individual needs, and selecting reputable exchanges with robust security measures, users can safeguard their digital assets and participate confidently in the cryptocurrency market.

Chapter 4: All about Bitcoin and Blockchain

Chapter introduction

Welcome to the comprehensive guide on Bitcoin and Blockchain. In this chapter, we will embark on an enlightening journey into the intricate world of digital currency and decentralized technology. Bitcoin, the pioneering cryptocurrency, and Blockchain, its underlying technology, have revolutionized the way we perceive and interact with money, transactions, and data.

From the fundamental concepts to advanced applications, we will explore every facet of Bitcoin and Blockchain, unraveling the mysteries behind their creation, operation, and impact on the global economy. Whether you're a newcomer curious about digital currencies or an experienced enthusiast seeking deeper insights, this chapter will equip you with the knowledge and understanding necessary to navigate the dynamic landscape of cryptocurrencies and decentralized systems.

Prepare to delve into the origins of Bitcoin, understand the principles of Blockchain technology, and explore the myriad possibilities that these innovations present. Join us as we embark on an illuminating exploration of all things Bitcoin and Blockchain.

Topic 21: Bitcoin explained in detail

In this section, we will delve into a detailed exploration of Bitcoin, uncovering its key features, functionalities, and implications. Bitcoin, the pioneering cryptocurrency, operates on the revolutionary technology known as blockchain. At its core, the Bitcoin blockchain is a decentralized and widely-shared ledger that records every transaction ever conducted with Bitcoin.

The blockchain of Bitcoin, like that of any other cryptocurrency, serves as a comprehensive and immutable record of all transactions. Spanning back to its inception in 2009, the Bitcoin blockchain has grown to be more than 200 GB in size, encompassing countless transactions from around the globe. Its colossal scale underscores the extensive adoption and usage of Bitcoin as a digital currency.

One of the defining characteristics of Bitcoin is its decentralized nature. Unlike traditional banking systems, Bitcoin transactions do not rely on intermediaries such as banks or credit card companies. Instead, transactions occur directly between peers, with no need for third-party involvement. This peer-to-peer model ensures greater autonomy and flexibility for users.

Anonymity is another hallmark of Bitcoin, offering users the ability to conduct transactions without revealing their identities. While Bitcoin transactions are theoretically anonymous, regulatory requirements may necessitate the disclosure of user identities on cryptocurrency exchanges. Nevertheless, the fundamental principle of anonymity remains a cornerstone of Bitcoin's ethos.

Central to Bitcoin's operation is the absence of a single trustee or central authority. Instead, Bitcoin transactions are validated and recorded by a network of thousands of computers worldwide. These computers, known as nodes, maintain a consensus on the validity of transactions through a process known as proof of work.

The tamper-proof nature of the Bitcoin blockchain is ensured through cryptographic mechanisms. Transactions recorded on the blockchain are encrypted and stored in blocks, making them impervious to tampering or alteration. The decentralized consensus mechanism further fortifies the integrity of the blockchain, ensuring that no single entity can manipulate the transaction records.

In essence, Bitcoin represents a paradigm shift in the realm of finance and technology. Its decentralized, secure, and transparent nature challenges traditional financial systems, offering a glimpse into the future of digital currency and decentralized finance. As we unravel the intricacies of Bitcoin, we gain a deeper understanding of its transformative potential and the vast opportunities it presents in the digital age.

Topic 22: Blockchain explained further

Bitcoin, often hailed as the pioneer of cryptocurrencies, operates on a revolutionary technology known as blockchain. To understand Bitcoin, it's crucial to grasp the intricacies of blockchain, which serves as the underlying framework for Bitcoin transactions.

At its core, blockchain is a shared ledger, akin to a giant list, that records every Bitcoin transaction ever made. This ledger is decentralized, meaning it is not controlled by any single entity but is shared among a vast network of computers worldwide.

The blockchain of Bitcoin is the largest among all cryptocurrencies, exceeding 200 GB in size. Each block in the blockchain is interconnected through cryptographic functions, creating a chain that is immutable and resistant to tampering. This cryptographic linkage ensures the integrity of the blockchain, making it virtually impossible to alter past transactions without detection.

Bitcoin transactions are validated and recorded through a process known as proof of work, which involves complex computational tasks. This proof of work mechanism ensures the authenticity of transactions and mitigates the risk of double spending, a key challenge in digital currency systems.

Decentralization lies at the heart of Bitcoin, with transactions occurring directly between peers without the need for intermediaries. This peer-to-peer model empowers users with greater autonomy and privacy, as transactions are conducted anonymously without the involvement of banks or financial institutions.

The decentralized nature of Bitcoin's blockchain ensures consensus among network participants, preventing any single user from controlling the ledger. This consensus-based verification mechanism safeguards the integrity and security of the Bitcoin network.

In essence, Bitcoin represents a paradigm shift in the world of finance, offering a decentralized alternative to traditional currency systems. Through blockchain technology, Bitcoin provides a transparent, secure, and efficient means of conducting financial transactions, paving the way for a new era of digital currency and decentralized finance.

Topic 23: Bitcoin verification process

The verification process of Bitcoin transactions is a critical component of the decentralized system, ensuring the integrity and security of the network. Let's delve deeper into how this process works to provide clarity on its intricacies.

At the heart of Bitcoin verification are professional verifiers, often referred to as Bitcoin miners. These miners play a crucial role in verifying transactions by dedicating computational power to solve complex mathematical puzzles, a process known as proof of work.

The verification process involves grouping transactions into blocks, with each block containing approximately 1200-1500 transaction data. Miners then compete to solve the mathematical puzzle associated with each block, aiming to guess a magic number based on cryptographic functions.

Once a miner successfully guesses the magic number and validates the block, it is added to the blockchain. In return for their efforts, miners receive a fixed number of bitcoins as a block reward. This reward, currently set at 12.5 bitcoins per block, is halved approximately every four years to control the supply of bitcoins.

The blockchain, essentially a chain of interconnected blocks, grows with each validated block, serving as a transparent and immutable ledger of all Bitcoin transactions. With an average block addition time of 10 minutes, miners work collaboratively to ensure the integrity and consensus of the network, preventing any single entity from controlling the verification process.

In essence, the verification process of Bitcoin transactions relies on the collective efforts of miners worldwide, reinforcing the decentralized nature of the network and ensuring the security and reliability of the digital currency system.

Topic 24: Role of Bitcoin miners

The role of Bitcoin miners is pivotal in ensuring the integrity and security of the blockchain network. Let's delve into their responsibilities to gain a clearer understanding.

Miners play a crucial role in extending the blockchain by attaching new blocks to the existing chain, thereby facilitating its continuous growth. Each block in the blockchain is intricately linked to all the preceding blocks through cryptographic functions, ensuring the immutability and integrity of the entire ledger.

The process of adding new blocks involves complex mathematical computations and cryptographic verification, ensuring that each block is genuine and uncompromised. Miners diligently work to prevent any tampering or manipulation of the blockchain, as any compromised block would render the entire chain invalid.

Invalid blocks, those that do not adhere to the cryptographic integrity of the chain, are swiftly identified and rejected by the Bitcoin network. Only valid blocks, verified by the majority of miners, are accepted and added to the blockchain, thereby maintaining the system's trustworthiness and reliability.

Central to the miner's role is the concept of proof of work, introduced by Satoshi Nakamoto to combat double spending and deter fraudulent activities. This mechanism makes it exceedingly challenging for fraudsters to add fake transactions to the blockchain, as only a minority of miners successfully guess the required cryptographic puzzle to validate new blocks.

The blockchain network operates on the principle of the longest verified chain, whereby the official version of the ledger is determined by the longest chain of valid blocks. Through constant communication and synchronization among network participants, the latest version of the blockchain is consistently updated and agreed upon, ensuring consensus and trust within the system.

In essence, Bitcoin miners serve as the backbone of the blockchain network, upholding its security, integrity, and decentralized nature through their diligent verification efforts and adherence to cryptographic principles.

Topic 25: Role of Bitcoin Software

The Bitcoin software plays a fundamental role in ensuring the smooth operation of the entire system, particularly in the mining process. Let's explore its key functions and significance in more detail.

At its core, the Bitcoin software is responsible for orchestrating the mining operation and maintaining the integrity of the blockchain. Its primary objective is to manage the system's needs, such as preventing double spending and regulating the addition of new blocks to the chain.

One of the most critical aspects of the software is its implementation of the proof-of-work mechanism, which serves to deter fraudulent activities and ensure the authenticity of transactions. Through sophisticated algorithms, the software adjusts the complexity of cryptographic puzzles based on the number of users actively participating in the network.

This dynamic adjustment of complexity is crucial for maintaining a consistent block addition rate of approximately 10 minutes. When user activity is high, the software increases the difficulty of solving cryptographic puzzles to ensure that blocks are added at a reasonable interval. Conversely, during periods of low activity, it reduces complexity to prevent excessive delays in block addition.

By striking this delicate balance, the Bitcoin software ensures a continuous flow of new verified blocks into the blockchain. This adaptability is essential as the network experiences constant fluctuations in the number of miners and their computing capabilities.

Furthermore, the software governs the release of block rewards, which incentivize miners to contribute their computational power to the network. Approximately every 10 minutes, a new block is added to the chain, accompanied by the issuance of a fixed number of bitcoins as a reward for the successful mining effort.

Over time, the supply of bitcoins is systematically controlled by the software, with the total number of coins capped at 21 million. This scarcity model, coupled with increasing demand, contributes to the appreciation of Bitcoin's value over time.

In summary, the Bitcoin software serves as the backbone of the network, orchestrating the mining process, regulating block addition, and ensuring the integrity and security of the blockchain. Its adaptive nature and meticulous management of resources are critical for the sustained operation and success of the Bitcoin ecosystem.

Chapter conclusion

In conclusion, our exploration of Bitcoin and blockchain technology has provided valuable insights into the intricacies of this revolutionary system. From understanding the basics of Bitcoin to delving into the role of miners and the Bitcoin software, we've gained a comprehensive understanding of how this decentralized digital currency operates.

Bitcoin's foundation lies in blockchain technology, a giant shared ledger that records every transaction in a tamper-proof and transparent manner. This blockchain is maintained and secured by a network of miners, who validate transactions through complex cryptographic puzzles.

The role of miners is crucial, as they ensure the authenticity of transactions and add new blocks to the blockchain at a consistent rate. Through the process of proof-of-work, miners compete to solve cryptographic puzzles, thereby verifying transactions and earning rewards in the form of bitcoins.

The Bitcoin software plays a pivotal role in orchestrating the mining process, adjusting the complexity of puzzles based on network activity, and regulating the issuance of new bitcoins. Its adaptability ensures the smooth functioning of the network, maintaining a steady flow of verified blocks while controlling the total supply of bitcoins over time.

As we've learned, Bitcoin's scarcity model, with a capped supply of 21 million coins, coupled with increasing demand, contributes to its value appreciation over time. This inherent scarcity, combined with its decentralized nature and security features, positions Bitcoin as a unique and valuable asset in the digital age.

In conclusion, our journey through the world of Bitcoin and blockchain has provided valuable insights into the mechanics and significance of this groundbreaking technology. As we continue to witness the evolution of cryptocurrencies and blockchain applications, it's clear that Bitcoin's impact on finance, technology, and society at large will continue to grow in the years to come.

Chapter 5: Economics of Bitcoin

Welcome to this chapter on the Economics of Bitcoin. In this chapter, we will delve into the fascinating world of cryptocurrency economics, focusing primarily on Bitcoin. As we stand on the cusp of a new era in global currencies, it's crucial to understand the pivotal role that Bitcoin and other cryptocurrencies play in shaping the future of finance.

Bitcoin, the pioneer of cryptocurrencies, has emerged as a disruptive force in the financial landscape, challenging traditional notions of money and value. Its meteoric rise in popularity and adoption has sparked widespread interest and debate, with proponents hailing it as the future of money and skeptics questioning its long-term viability.

Throughout this chapter, we will explore the reasons behind Bitcoin's remarkable ascent, examining the economic principles that underpin its value proposition. From its decentralized nature to its limited supply and deflationary model, we will uncover the key factors driving Bitcoin's rise as a digital gold and store of value.

Furthermore, we will analyze the broader economic implications of Bitcoin's emergence, considering its impact on monetary policy, financial markets, and the global economy. As governments and central banks grapple with unprecedented economic challenges, Bitcoin offers a compelling alternative that promises greater financial autonomy and censorship resistance.

Join us as we unravel the economics of Bitcoin and navigate the complex terrain of cryptocurrency in the quest for a decentralized and borderless financial future.

Topic 26: Three eras of world currencies

Welcome back to this book, where we delve into all things Bitcoin and Blockchain. In our previous episodes, we explored the intricacies of Blockchain technology, the verification process of Bitcoin, the crucial role of miners, and the functions of Bitcoin software. Today, we embark on a journey into the realm of international macroeconomics, particularly focusing on the history and evolution of world currencies.

Throughout history, currencies have undergone significant transformations, reflecting changes in economic systems, trade dynamics, and geopolitical landscapes. Broadly, we can identify three distinct eras of currencies: the commodities-based era, the gold standard era, and the political-based era.

In the **commodities-based era**, various commodities such as spices, stones, and rare metals like gold and silver served as currency. These commodities facilitated trade and economic transactions, providing a medium of exchange in local and international commerce.

The **gold standard era** emerged as a dominant force in international transactions, especially before World War I. Gold, with its intrinsic value and universal acceptance, became the standard for assessing the value of currencies. However, the aftermath of World War I and World War II led to a loss of faith in the gold standard, paving the way for a new era.

The **political-based era**, also known as the dollar economy, gained prominence post-World War II. The US Dollar emerged as the apex currency in global transactions, dominating the international foreign exchange market with over 80% of transactions conducted in dollars.

In subsequent episodes, we will delve deeper into the dynamics of this political-based era, exploring the role of the US Dollar and its implications for global economics. Additionally, we will examine where Bitcoin and other cryptocurrencies fit into this evolving landscape, offering insights into their potential impact on the future of world currencies.

Join us as we unravel the fascinating history of world currencies and navigate the complex interplay between tradition and innovation in the realm of global finance.

In the realm of world currencies, we've witnessed the dominance of the dollar economy, where the US Dollar reigns supreme, accounting for a staggering 80% share in global transactions. However, a new era has dawned – the era of mathematical currency.

This mathematical currency, epitomized by cryptocurrencies like Bitcoin, Ethereum, and Litecoin, represents a paradigm shift from traditional commodities and politically-backed currencies. Born out of advancements in information and communication technology, this digital currency operates on the principles of cryptography, making it decentralized, digital, and intangible.

With over 7,000 cryptocurrencies currently in existence and Bitcoin alone commanding a market share of 50%, the cryptocurrency market boasts a total value approaching 1 trillion dollars. This exponential growth begs the question: is it sustainable? Does it have a future?

Many experts argue that cryptocurrencies are not just a passing trend but a revolutionary force poised to reshape the future of currency. As blockchain technology, the underlying framework of cryptocurrencies, finds applications beyond just currency, its significance only grows.

While the possibility of an intergalactic currency may seem like science fiction, one thing is certain: if such a need arises in the future, it will likely be rooted in the principles of mathematics and physics, much like cryptocurrency is today.

As we explore the economics of Bitcoin and its role in the global currency market, it becomes evident that we stand on the cusp of a transformative era in finance. With each passing day, cryptocurrencies edge closer to mainstream acceptance, promising a future where digital currencies may indeed reign supreme.

Join us as we delve deeper into the economics of Bitcoin and unlock the secrets of this groundbreaking currency in the episodes to come.

Topic 27: 200 Million $ Pizza Problem: An interesting case study on the rise of Bitcoin

Let me share an intriguing story with you – one that has become a legend in the world of Bitcoin. It's known as the "$70 Million Pizza Problem" and offers a fascinating glimpse into the rise of Bitcoin.

Back in 2010, in a Florida forum, a user named LajLo Hani made a seemingly innocent proposition: he offered 10,000 bitcoins to anyone willing to order him a pizza. At the time, the value of 10,000 bitcoins was around $40-41 – a trivial sum in today's context. However, a British citizen took up the challenge and ordered a pizza for Hani, who duly transferred the 10,000 bitcoins.

Now, here's where the story takes a jaw-dropping turn. Those 10,000 bitcoins, once worth a mere $40-41, are now valued at over $100 million. Yes, you read that right – more than $100 million! This remarkable appreciation in value over just a decade has left many scratching their heads and questioning the nature of Bitcoin's meteoric rise.

What's particularly intriguing is that even with this astronomical value, you still can't stroll into a pizza joint and buy yourself a pie with bitcoins. While some international organizations now accept Bitcoin, it's still far from mainstream use. This tale highlights the complexities and challenges associated with using Bitcoin in everyday transactions.

So why is it called the "$70 Million Pizza Problem"? Well, because even though the pizza bought with those 10,000 bitcoins is now worth around $100 million, you still can't simply use bitcoins to buy a pizza. It's a quirky reminder of Bitcoin's journey from novelty to financial juggernaut.

This story offers a glimpse into the unique ecosystem of Bitcoin and the intricacies involved in its adoption and use. Join me as we delve deeper into the fascinating world of cryptocurrencies and uncover the lessons hidden within this remarkable tale.

Let's delve deeper into the "$200 Million Pizza Problem" and uncover another facet of Bitcoin's remarkable journey – its sustainability.

As we discussed earlier, the trajectory of Bitcoin's rise seems almost unbelievable. But behind this exponential growth lies a crucial mechanism: the halving of Bitcoin rewards every four years. This means that the number of bitcoins entering the market decreases over time, with the reward for mining a block being halved. By 2140, the reward will hit zero, marking the issuance of 99% of the total 21 million bitcoins.

Now, here's where things get interesting. The motivation for mining Bitcoin hinges on its rising value. As we've witnessed, Bitcoin's price has soared to impressive heights, reaching $13-14,000 per Bitcoin. But what happens if this trajectory falters? If Bitcoin's value stagnates or declines, the entire system could be at risk.

Mining Bitcoin requires significant computational power, which translates to high energy costs. The sprawling rigs housing thousands of computers consume vast amounts of electricity, raising concerns about environmental impact. If the value of Bitcoin fails to justify these energy-intensive processes, the economics of Bitcoin could collapse.

This presents a daunting challenge. If the exponential rise in Bitcoin's value stalls, miners may lose their motivation to verify transactions. Without verification, the system's core feature – double spending avoidance – would be compromised. This dark side of Bitcoin underscores the inherent risks associated with its sustainability.

Understanding these complexities is crucial for investors and enthusiasts alike. While Bitcoin's rise has been meteoric, its future hinges on maintaining momentum. If this momentum wanes, the consequences could be dire for those heavily invested in the cryptocurrency.

Join me as we explore the intricate dynamics of Bitcoin's sustainability and unravel the mysteries of its future trajectory.

Topic 28: Bitcoins Mining Operations

Bitcoin mining operations are a cornerstone of the cryptocurrency ecosystem, but they're far from simple. In fact, solo mining – the idea of an individual computer tackling the immense computational requirements – is virtually impossible. With an average time of 57 years to complete the necessary work for a single block, the motivation simply isn't there.

Instead, mining pools are essential. These pools bring together vast computational and hashing power from hundreds or thousands of computers, all networked and communicating via internet technology. But with such collective power comes significant energy usage. It's a natural consequence of the networked computers constantly communicating and calculating.

Mining pools effectively combine computational power – for mathematical computations – with hashing power, for guessing the correct hash. And within these pools, earnings are distributed among participants, much like splitting the costs of a party among friends. It's a cooperative effort, ensuring that everyone shares in both the costs and the rewards.

However, the logistics of managing individual computers within a pool can be daunting. Enter cloud mining – a newer concept that offers a solution. With cloud mining, individuals can leverage shared computational and hashing power without the need for personal equipment. It's a more practical approach, particularly given the immense computational demands and the associated costs and opportunity costs of running individual machines.

Stay with me as we delve deeper into the intricacies of Bitcoin mining operations and explore how these pools and cloud mining are shaping the landscape of cryptocurrency mining.

In the world of Bitcoin mining operations, cloud mining has emerged as a game-changer. But what exactly is cloud mining, and why is it gaining traction?

Cloud mining involves investing in specialized mining rigs operated by corporate entities. These rigs are massive, factory-like setups equipped with ASIC-based hardware, specifically designed for Bitcoin mining. ASIC (Application-Specific Integrated Circuit) technology is at the forefront of this innovation, primarily centered in China where manufacturing and usage are most prevalent.

So, how does cloud mining work? Instead of purchasing and maintaining your own equipment, cloud mining allows individuals to become investors in these large-scale operations. By investing through cloud mining platforms, you participate in the collective expenditure of these billion-dollar facilities.

One key reason for the success of cloud mining lies in its efficiency. Unlike individual mining or even mining pools, cloud mining operations benefit from economies of scale and optimized energy usage. These facilities are strategically located in areas with cheap electricity, often utilizing coal or geothermal energy sources. Additionally, the cold climate in places like Iceland naturally cools the equipment, reducing energy needs further.

The result? Cloud mining offers higher returns on investment compared to individual mining or even traditional mining pools. With 80% of Bitcoins mined in China, these cloud mining operations dominate the landscape, thanks to their efficiency and scale.

So, if you're considering Bitcoin mining, cloud mining offers the most practical

Topic 29: Dark sides of CRYPTOs

Cryptocurrencies, including Bitcoin, have undoubtedly revolutionized finance and technology. However, like any innovation, they too have their dark sides. Let's delve into some of the key concerns surrounding cryptocurrencies, shedding light on their potential pitfalls.

Firstly, consider the environmental impact of Bitcoin mining. The immense computational power required for mining operations consumes vast amounts of electricity, contributing to climate change and environmental degradation. With thousands of cryptocurrencies in existence and their usage on the rise, this energy-intensive process raises serious sustainability questions for our planet's future.

Moreover, the very foundation of cryptocurrencies, particularly Bitcoin, lies in their decentralized nature facilitated by blockchain technology. However, the sheer size of the blockchain, exceeding 200 GB for Bitcoin alone, presents a significant challenge. Maintaining a full node, essential for ensuring decentralization and network integrity, becomes increasingly impractical as the blockchain grows. This dilemma leads to the emergence of lighter nodes, compromising the decentralization ethos and diluting consensus within the network.

Additionally, the allure of quick profits and speculative trading in the cryptocurrency market poses risks for investors. The volatile nature of cryptocurrency prices, coupled with regulatory uncertainties and market manipulation, underscores the inherent instability and unpredictability of this burgeoning asset class.

Furthermore, the anonymity afforded by cryptocurrencies has fostered illicit activities on the dark web, ranging from money laundering and drug trafficking to cybercrime and terrorism financing. Despite efforts to regulate and monitor these activities, the decentralized and pseudonymous nature of cryptocurrencies presents ongoing challenges for law enforcement and regulatory authorities.

In conclusion, while cryptocurrencies offer promising opportunities for innovation and financial inclusion, they also harbor significant risks and challenges. Addressing these dark sides requires a balanced approach that promotes innovation while safeguarding against environmental harm, financial instability, and criminal exploitation. As we navigate the evolving landscape of cryptocurrencies, vigilance, regulation, and responsible investment practices are essential to mitigate risks and ensure a sustainable future for this disruptive technology.

When we examine the dark sides of cryptocurrencies, particularly Bitcoin, several concerning issues come to light. Let's explore these challenges and their implications for the future of digital currencies.

Firstly, the concept of decentralization, a cornerstone of cryptocurrencies, is increasingly under threat. With the concentration of computational power in the hands of a select few, the very essence of decentralization is compromised. Cloud mining, where large corporations control significant mining rigs, exacerbates this issue, allowing a privileged few to dominate the network and potentially manipulate blockchain transactions.

Moreover, the prevalence of a single software, Bitcoin Core Software, used by 97% of miners, raises alarm bells. With a small group of individuals possessing comprehensive knowledge of this software, there's a risk of centralization and manipulation, undermining the decentralized ethos of Bitcoin.

Additionally, the dominance of a few Chinese companies in innovating ASIC hardware, specialized for Bitcoin mining, poses a significant threat to decentralization. With a market share of 70 to 80%, these companies wield immense control over the hardware crucial for mining operations. This concentration of power not only enables potential 51% attacks but also undermines the decentralized nature of Bitcoin, as control shifts to a select few.

Furthermore, the consolidation of mining rigs and pools in the hands of a handful of companies further exacerbates centralization concerns. These companies, often associated with ASIC manufacturing giants, monopolize the majority of Bitcoin mining, consolidating control and potentially endangering the integrity of the network.

While these dark sides of Bitcoin have yet to manifest in major crises, they represent significant vulnerabilities that could threaten the stability and trustworthiness of the cryptocurrency ecosystem. Understanding these challenges is crucial for ensuring informed decision-making and safeguarding against potential risks in the evolving landscape of digital currencies.

Chapter conclusion

In conclusion, the exploration of the dark sides of cryptocurrencies, particularly focusing on Bitcoin, reveals a series of significant challenges that threaten the fundamental principles of decentralization and trust within the digital currency ecosystem.

From the concentration of computational power in the hands of a privileged few to the dominance of a single software and the monopolization of ASIC hardware by select Chinese companies, the decentralized ethos of Bitcoin faces mounting threats. The emergence of cloud mining and the consolidation of mining rigs and pools further exacerbate centralization concerns, posing risks of manipulation and 51% attacks.

While these dark sides have yet to materialize into major crises, they underscore the importance of vigilance and informed decision-making in navigating the complexities of the cryptocurrency landscape. As the adoption of digital currencies continues to grow, addressing these vulnerabilities becomes imperative to safeguard the integrity and sustainability of the entire ecosystem.

Moving forward, stakeholders must remain vigilant, advocating for transparency, decentralization, and inclusivity to mitigate the risks posed by centralization and manipulation. By fostering an environment of collaboration, innovation, and accountability, we can navigate the dark sides of cryptocurrencies and pave the way for a more resilient and trustworthy digital financial future.

Discussion Questions

1. How do the potential risks and dark sides associated with cryptocurrencies discussed in the previous chapter impact the adoption and implementation of blockchain technology in business applications, as outlined in the subsequent chapter?

2. Reflecting on the discussion of cryptocurrencies in the previous chapter, how do you think the principles of decentralization and transparency inherent in blockchain technology can mitigate some of the challenges posed by centralized financial systems?

3. Considering the applications of blockchain technology discussed in the subsequent chapter, such as smart contracts and smart supply chains, how might these innovations address the environmental concerns raised regarding the energy-intensive nature of cryptocurrency mining?

4. Building on the discussion of IoT-based smart properties and smart supply chains, how might the integration of blockchain technology enhance transparency and trust in global trade and commerce, particularly in sectors like manufacturing and logistics?

5. In light of the potential benefits of blockchain technology for improving data security and privacy, as discussed in the subsequent chapter, how might businesses and organizations leverage blockchain solutions to enhance cybersecurity measures and protect sensitive information?

6. Reflecting on the regulatory considerations raised in the subsequent chapter, how do you think policymakers can balance the need for innovation and technological advancement with the imperative to ensure consumer protection and regulatory compliance in the blockchain space?

7. Considering the implications of blockchain-based identity management discussed in the subsequent chapter, how might decentralized identity solutions address concerns related to data breaches and identity theft in digital transactions and online services?

8.   Building on the discussion of financial inclusion and access to banking services in the subsequent chapter, how might blockchain technology be leveraged to bridge the gap between the unbanked population and traditional financial systems, particularly in developing regions?

9.   Reflecting on the potential impact of blockchain technology on traditional banking and financial institutions, as discussed in the subsequent chapter, how might these institutions adapt their business models and services to remain competitive in the era of decentralized finance (DeFi) and tokenization of assets?

10. Considering the broader societal implications of blockchain technology discussed in both chapters, how might blockchain innovations contribute to economic development, social empowerment, and global sustainability goals in the years to come?

Chapter 6: Business Applications of Blockchain Technology

Welcome to the next chapter, where we delve into the fascinating realm of blockchain technology and its myriad business applications. From enhancing supply chain management to revolutionizing financial transactions, blockchain has the potential to transform our everyday lives in remarkable ways.

In this chapter, we will explore the innovative products and solutions powered by blockchain technology that are reshaping industries and driving forward-thinking businesses towards unprecedented levels of efficiency, transparency, and security. Whether it's streamlining cross-border payments, enabling smart contracts, or ensuring the authenticity of products through immutable ledgers, blockchain is unlocking new possibilities across various sectors.

Join me as we unravel the exciting world of blockchain-powered solutions and discover how they are poised to revolutionize the way we conduct business, interact with technology, and navigate the digital landscape. From decentralized finance (DeFi) platforms to supply chain traceability solutions, the potential of blockchain knows no bounds, and the possibilities are truly endless. Let's embark on this journey together and explore the transformative power of blockchain technology in shaping the future of business.

Topic 30: Blockchain Projects

Welcome back to the book, where we dive into the world of blockchain and its practical applications in business. In our previous discussion, we explored the intricacies of Bitcoin economics and the unique features of cryptocurrencies. Today, we shift our focus towards understanding how blockchain technology can be harnessed to create innovative business solutions.

One fundamental aspect to grasp is the close relationship between blockchain and cryptocurrencies. In fact, most blockchain applications are inextricably linked to some form of cryptocurrency. Without this association, standalone blockchain applications cannot be developed. This underscores the vital role of cryptocurrencies as the backbone of blockchain-based projects.

When launching a blockchain project, financing plays a crucial role. Traditionally, raising capital for startups follows conventional routes. However, in the realm of blockchain, fundraising is intricately tied to cryptocurrencies. Enter tokens – the lifeline of blockchain projects. These tokens come in two primary forms: security tokens and utility tokens.

Security tokens function akin to company shares, enabling project owners to raise capital by offering them in the market. On the other hand, utility tokens serve a different purpose. They provide early adopters with access to future products and services offered by the project. While both tokens operate as currencies in the market, utility tokens differ in that they do not have their own blockchain. Instead, they leverage existing blockchain platforms for functionality.

In essence, tokens represent a new paradigm in fundraising, born from the cryptocurrency concept. As we delve deeper into blockchain projects, we'll explore how these tokens are leveraged to drive innovation, create value for customers, and revolutionize various industries. Join me as we unravel the complexities and potentials of blockchain-based business applications in the chapters to come.

In the realm of blockchain projects, the concept of tokens takes center stage. These tokens serve as the cornerstone of innovative business applications, tightly woven into the fabric of blockchain technology. Without the token system, many of these applications would simply not find a foothold in the business landscape. So, let's delve deeper into this concept.

Tokens represent a new frontier in cryptocurrency, operating as a next-level iteration of digital currency. Much like Bitcoin, tokens can be traded in the market, bought, and sold with relative ease. But what sets tokens apart is their close association with blockchain applications.

When discussing blockchain applications, it's crucial to understand that most are intricately connected with some form of cryptocurrency, like Bitcoin. One of the most significant applications of blockchain technology is Blockchain Finance. Here, we witness a plethora of innovative projects and startups pioneering new financial solutions.

Take Ethereum, for instance. This sophisticated cryptocurrency boasts a robust blockchain platform, complete with smart contract capabilities. Leveraging Ethereum's platform, individuals and organizations have launched a myriad of financial products, issuing tokens that have garnered significant popularity and investment.

These financial products span a wide array of offerings, including asset management solutions and smart insurance products within the insurance sector. Additionally, blockchain technology has revolutionized cross-border payments, exemplified by the issuance of blockchain-based letters of credit. Just recently, HSBC Bank in Bangladesh issued the first blockchain-based letter of credit, dramatically reducing processing times from days to a mere 24 hours.

Furthermore, the realm of decentralized finance (DeFi) is gaining momentum. DeFi encompasses a range of financial products, including lending solutions, all powered by blockchain technology. Investments in DeFi tokens are skyrocketing, surpassing even the popularity of traditional cryptocurrencies.

In essence, the rise of blockchain-based financial products underscores the transformative potential of blockchain technology. As we explore further into this chapter, we'll uncover more groundbreaking projects and delve into the myriad opportunities blockchain offers in the realm of business applications.

Topic 31: IoT based smart properties

In the ever-evolving landscape of blockchain applications, one area that stands out is IoT-based smart properties. This innovative concept entails linking tangible and intangible properties to the internet, assigning them unique codes, and making them blockchain compliant. Once connected to the internet and blockchain, these properties undergo a transformation into digital assets, opening up a realm of possibilities for online trading and smart property contracts.

Smart properties are at the forefront of decentralized finance (DeFi), offering a bridge between the physical and digital worlds. Through blockchain technology, projects have emerged to convert various assets, such as real estate and machinery, into smart properties. For instance, an entire office building can be divided into units, categorized, and linked to the internet, each unit assigned a unique code and transformed into a digital asset.

Consider the example of a factory equipped with machinery linked to the internet via unique codes. Through IoT-based smart management, the factory can automate inventory tracking, maintenance scheduling, and part replacements. By harnessing the power of blockchain algorithms and artificial intelligence, the need for human intervention is minimized, ensuring efficient management of equipment and devices on a large scale.

Moreover, IoT-based smart properties extend beyond industrial settings to consumer goods. Manufacturers can utilize blockchain-enabled IoT to provide customers with real-time information about product lifespan, warranty status, and potential issues. This proactive approach to customer relations management enhances consumer satisfaction and loyalty.

In essence, IoT-based smart properties represent a convergence of blockchain technology and the Internet of Things, revolutionizing how we manage assets and devices in both commercial and consumer spheres. As we explore further into this chapter, we'll uncover more innovative applications of blockchain in business, driving efficiency, transparency, and value creation across various industries.

Topic 32: Smart Supply Chains

In the realm of blockchain applications, one of the most impactful innovations is seen in the domain of international logistics and supply chain management. This transformative concept involves leveraging the Internet of Things (IoT) to track and manage global shipments, be it goods or services, using blockchain algorithms and artificial intelligence.

Through the integration of smart sensors into shipment containers and linking them to the internet with unique codes, smart supply chain projects have emerged. These initiatives enable real-time tracking of shipments and seamless management through blockchain algorithms, which operate based on predefined terms and conditions agreed upon with clients.

By harnessing the power of blockchain and IoT, businesses can optimize supply chain operations, minimize losses and damages, and enhance overall efficiency. Moreover, smart supply chains offer the potential to streamline international logistics processes, saving time and reducing costs.

The market for smart supply chain projects is burgeoning, with numerous opportunities for growth and expansion. Through tokenization, these projects can be introduced to the market, gaining popularity and achieving scalability on a global scale.

In summary, smart supply chains represent a significant advancement in logistics and supply chain management, paving the way for improved transparency, efficiency, and cost-effectiveness in international trade. As businesses continue to embrace blockchain technology, the future of supply chain management looks increasingly promising.

Topic 33: Smart eCommerce

In the realm of e-commerce, there's a revolutionary concept gaining traction known as smart contracts. These contracts, based on principles like If This Then That (IFTTT), have the potential to transform the landscape of international commerce and large-scale transactions.

Smart contracts operate on pre-defined rules and algorithms agreed upon by parties involved. They offer a streamlined approach to handling transactions, significantly reducing costs, time, and disputes. By automating processes and ensuring adherence to agreed terms, smart contracts mitigate uncertainty and minimize the need for arbitration.

The applications of smart contracts in commerce are vast and promising. They hold the key to unlocking efficiency and transparency in transactions on a massive scale. As blockchain technology continues to evolve, we can expect to see a surge in the adoption of smart contracts in various industries, propelling e-commerce into a new era of efficiency and reliability.

With the increasing popularity of decentralized finance (DeFi) products and the emergence of related tokens, the potential of blockchain technology is brighter than ever. As more businesses recognize the benefits of smart contracts, we anticipate a surge in their adoption and integration into mainstream commerce.

In conclusion, smart contracts represent a significant leap forward in the world of e-commerce, offering unparalleled efficiency, transparency, and security. As the technology matures, we can look forward to a future where smart contracts play a central role in facilitating seamless transactions across the global marketplace.

Chapter Conclusion

In conclusion, the potential of blockchain technology in revolutionizing various aspects of business, particularly in areas like finance, supply chain management, and e-commerce, is undeniable. Through applications like decentralized finance (DeFi), smart contracts, and Internet of Things (IoT) integration, blockchain offers solutions that enhance efficiency, transparency, and security in commercial transactions.

By leveraging blockchain technology, businesses can streamline processes, reduce costs, mitigate risks, and improve customer experiences. The advent of DeFi products, smart contracts, and IoT-based solutions opens up new possibilities for innovation and growth in the global marketplace.

As we move forward, it's clear that blockchain will continue to play a pivotal role in shaping the future of commerce. With ongoing advancements and increasing adoption, businesses stand to benefit immensely from harnessing the power of blockchain technology to drive their operations forward.

In summary, the potential of blockchain technology to transform business operations is vast and promising. By embracing blockchain-based solutions, businesses can position themselves for success in an increasingly digital and interconnected world.

Discussion Questions

1. How do you think decentralized finance (DeFi) products can revolutionize traditional financial systems? What are some potential benefits and challenges associated with their adoption?

2. Discuss the role of smart contracts in reducing inefficiencies and disputes in e-commerce and international commerce. How can smart contracts streamline business transactions and improve trust between parties?

3. What are the implications of integrating Internet of Things (IoT) technology with blockchain for supply chain management? How can smart supply chains enhance transparency, traceability, and efficiency in logistics operations?

4. In what ways can blockchain technology address challenges related to data security and privacy in online transactions? How do you envision blockchain-based solutions impacting cybersecurity in the future?

5.   Explore the concept of tokenization of assets and its significance in the context of smart properties and smart contracts. How can tokenization unlock liquidity, facilitate investment, and enable fractional ownership of assets?

6.   Discuss the potential impact of blockchain technology on traditional banking and financial institutions. How might these institutions adapt to the rise of DeFi and other blockchain-based innovations?

7.   Consider the environmental implications of blockchain mining operations, particularly in terms of energy consumption and carbon emissions. What measures can be taken to mitigate the environmental footprint of blockchain technology?

8.   How do you see the regulatory landscape evolving in response to the growing adoption of blockchain technology? What are some key considerations for policymakers in balancing innovation with regulatory oversight?

9.   Explore the concept of blockchain-based identity management and its potential applications in various industries, including healthcare, finance, and government services. What are some opportunities and challenges associated with decentralized identity solutions?

10.   Reflect on the role of blockchain technology in promoting financial inclusion and access to banking services, especially in underserved communities and developing countries. What are some initiatives leveraging blockchain for social impact and economic empowerment?

Book Conclusion

In conclusion, this book has delved into the fascinating world of blockchain technology and its myriad applications across various industries. From its humble origins as the underlying technology behind cryptocurrencies like Bitcoin to its potential to revolutionize supply chain management, finance, and beyond, blockchain has emerged as a transformative force in the digital age.

Throughout the chapters, we have explored both the promises and challenges of blockchain technology. On one hand, its decentralized nature offers the potential for increased transparency, efficiency, and security in transactions. It holds the promise of democratizing access to financial services, streamlining supply chains, and unlocking new opportunities for innovation and economic empowerment.

However, we have also confronted the dark sides of blockchain, including environmental concerns associated with cryptocurrency mining, regulatory uncertainties, and ethical considerations surrounding data privacy and security. These challenges underscore the need for responsible innovation, thoughtful regulation, and ongoing dialogue among stakeholders to ensure that blockchain technology realizes its full potential for positive impact while mitigating potential risks.

Looking ahead, the future of blockchain remains bright but uncertain. As the technology continues to evolve and mature, it will be essential for businesses, policymakers, and society as a whole to navigate these complexities collaboratively. By fostering innovation, promoting education and digital literacy, and embracing ethical principles, we can harness the transformative power of blockchain to build a more inclusive, transparent, and resilient digital economy for generations to come.

Topic 34: Concluding reamarks of the author

In concluding this Mastery Series on Bitcoin and Blockchain, it's evident that we've covered significant ground in understanding the fundamentals and potential applications of this groundbreaking technology. Throughout our journey, we've explored the basics of Bitcoin, delved into the intricacies of blockchain, and examined its wide-ranging implications across various industries.

As we wrap up, it's essential to recognize that blockchain holds immense promise for the future. It's not just about Bitcoin; it's about the transformative power of decentralized, transparent, and secure digital ledgers. The projections for blockchain's growth are staggering, with estimates suggesting a multi-trillion-dollar industry by 2030.

For those embarking on this journey, now is indeed the opportune moment. Just as pioneers capitalized on the early days of the internet, there's a similar window of opportunity with blockchain. Whether in finance, supply chain management, healthcare, or beyond, the potential for innovation and disruption is vast.

Moreover, the landscape is evolving rapidly, with major players like IBM and Deloitte leading the charge. This underscores the importance of staying informed, exploring new ideas, and leveraging blockchain technology to its fullest potential.

So, as we conclude this series, I encourage you to dive deeper into blockchain, explore its applications, and seize the opportunities that lie ahead. With the right knowledge, vision, and determination, the possibilities are limitless in this dynamic and ever-evolving field.

As we draw to a close on this Mastery Series, I want to emphasize the incredible opportunities that lie ahead in the world of blockchain and cryptocurrency. It's not just about understanding the technology; it's about seizing the moment and turning ideas into reality.

The timing couldn't be more perfect. With blockchain poised to revolutionize industries from finance to healthcare to governance, there's no shortage of avenues for innovation. And the best part? The resources and information you need to succeed are right at your fingertips.

Whether it's connecting with international organizations, sharing your ideas, or collaborating with like-minded individuals, now is the time to act. Blockchain isn't just a buzzword; it's a game-changer with the potential to shape the future in profound ways.

I hope this course has provided you with the knowledge and inspiration to embark on your blockchain journey. Remember, the possibilities are limitless, and with dedication and ingenuity, you can be at the forefront of this transformative technology.

Thank you for joining me on this enlightening journey, and remember to keep exploring, keep innovating, and keep pushing the boundaries of what's possible with blockchain and cryptocurrency.

ABOUT THE AUTHOR

Dr. Vijesh Jain is *a corporate trainer, management consultant, and instructor of* VJ Export Mastery Courses Series on UDEMY. He has written more than 10 books on export and import related topics. These books are available on Amazom and Kindle. He already has more than a quarter million of student enrollments on Udemy. He is an MIB, IIFT, New Delhi, B.E.BITS, Pilani, Phd from University of Mysore and a Certified Global Business Professional by NASBITE, USA. He is the first ever recipient of the best PhD thesis award conferred by BIMTECH, Delhi NCR. He has also contributed several research papers, those are published in top international research journals. He is the pioneer research scientist in the area of cross cultural management research, having postulated CFC dimension of world cultures. He is widely travelled abroad, having worked with top multinational companies involved in global business and has attended several international conferences and presented papers there. He has trained 1000s of working executives in India and abroad in the area of Global Management, Foreign Trade, Blockchain and Metaverse applications in international trade operations. With a total work experience of more than 35 years with global companies, he has also worked as Dean/Director with several reputed B Schools.